SCHOLASTIC

Using Picture Books to Teach
Narrative Writing

Engaging Mini-Lessons and Activities to
Teach Students About Key Story Elements

Naomi Laker

New York • Toronto • London • Auckland • Sydney
Mexico City • New Delhi • Hong Kong • Buenos Aires

Teaching *Resources*

DEDICATION

In loving memory of Oscar—the most wonderful cat and the best material for all of my stories
For Leo and Scott—my greatest loves and my biggest fans.
It's because of both of you that I smile every day.

ACKNOWLEDGMENTS

Teaching writing is always challenging and exciting. Helping children find "the" story to put down on paper is one of the most satisfying moments in a writing workshop. I have been lucky to share many of these moments with the children who have passed through my classroom at P.S. 41 in Manhattan. Each one of them has enriched my life as a teacher and as a person. They have taught me lessons about patience, trust, dedication, and achievement. A million thanks and much love to all of them. I believe that all children have the potential to be great writers—they just need to believe in themselves.

Teacher's College at Columbia University changed my life as a teacher and made it possible for me to have those magical moments in writing workshop. The guidance and inspiration I received from the summer institutes, workshops, leadership group, and staff developers are immeasurable. Special thanks to Patty Vitale and Carl Anderson, who spent many days in my classroom showing me how it's done.

Of course being a teacher is not an independent job. I would not be the teacher I am today if it weren't for the staff and administration I had at P.S. 41. To all of the teachers who have let me into their classrooms to share, plan, and model—thank you isn't enough. Your trust and belief in me made working with you an experience I will never forget. I am especially grateful to Kelly Shannon for her never-ending support, to Florence Roen for being a fantastic role model, and to Jennifer Korten, Stacey Miller, Debbie Flaum, John Baird, Jill Simon, Karen O'Neill, and Frances Schuchman for being more than colleagues, but friends as well.

Special thanks to Maria Chang of Scholastic for "discovering" me when she was my class parent and giving me the chance to share what I know about writing with others. And many thanks to Merryl Maleska Wilbur, my development editor. I had no idea what it meant to edit a book until Merryl came along and held my hand through the whole process.

Lastly, my success in my career would not have been possible if it weren't for the unconditional love and support from my family and friends. I am surrounded by love and inspiration—nothing makes a better teacher than that!

Cover design by Maria Lilja
Interior design by Russell Cohen
Photographs provided by Naomi Laker and James Levin Studio

ISBN 0-439-51379-0
Copyright © 2006 by Naomi Laker
All rights reserved.
Printed in the USA.

1 2 3 4 5 6 7 8 9 10 40 12 11 10 09 08 07 06

Contents

Introduction

As a teacher, one of the goals closest to my heart is to create young writers who enjoy writing and who feel confident in their abilities as writers. To that end, I've developed this particular unit of study that includes both a reading and a writing workshop to give my students the skills and confidence to try new types of writing.

In this unit of study, young readers and writers tackle many new tasks. Here they write, often for the first time, a fluent story with a clear beginning, middle, and end. We ask children to call on their own lives to write a personal narrative because this is the most natural place for them to begin and because this type of writing is easiest for them. Within this context, and using carefully selected narrative picture books as models, we ask children to choose a topic, create a plan for their narrative, use elaboration strategies, draft a story that will hold the reader's interest, edit, revise, and, finally, publish.

How to Use This Book

Each chapter in this book covers a week or several weeks' lessons in this nine-week unit of study. (Feel free to adjust the lessons according to your timeframe.) Each chapter opens with a planning calendar for the targeted week(s). The calendar lists the goals for all lessons—both instructional and review—for each day of the week, allowing you to see at a glance what the entire week looks like. I find these calendars very helpful. They organize my teaching and keep me on track with my lessons.

Within the chapter, each lesson offers directions for conducting the lesson, both descriptively and through sample dialogue. The lessons are transcribed from my own classroom (so I know that they really work!). You'll find samples of children's work along with each lesson where applicable.

Setting the Context: Reading and Writing Workshops

The unit begins with a three-week reading workshop, set up to familiarize children with the key narrative story elements as represented in three excellent picture books that you read aloud and discuss in depth as a class. As Joanne Hindley explains in *In the Company of Children* (1996), exploring a genre of literature as a whole class in this focused manner is an excellent means of encouraging children to use what they have learned in their own projects.

Once children are thoroughly acquainted with the story elements and have developed a real sense of what makes a story a story, they are ready to begin the writing workshop core of the unit. During the next four weeks you model your own story while children write the first draft of a well-structured personal narrative that incorporates the key story elements. In the final two weeks of the unit, children revise and edit their work and, finally, copy it over, illustrate it, and publish it to share with the world.

Using Model Books to Help Students Understand Narrative Writing

I always think of the reading workshop as the place to start a writing unit. That's because the first step in teaching children to write personal narratives is to give them a strong understanding of what a narrative is. Only after several weeks of being immersed in stories can children come to truly understand the characteristics of narrative writing. As teachers of writing, we must encourage our students to look at published text as models for their own writing (Ray, 2002).

We use picture books because these are already such a central part of young children's experiences with literacy. Children use picture books to become more fluent readers, to understand concepts of print, and to learn the key aspects of storytelling. Picture books are a young reader's glimpse into the world of writing as well (Calkins, 2001). From repeated exposure to high-quality picture books, children learn how writing looks and sounds. They make interpretations and engage their imagination, envisioning and embellishing on characters. What an opportunity this presents for challenging children to write good stories themselves. "Every act of reading, then, can essentially be an act of curriculum development for us as teachers of writing. Every single text we encounter represents a whole chunk of curriculum, a whole set of things to know about writing" (Ray, 2002).

Children usually love picture books of all varieties, but the focus in this unit is on one specific genre—narrative writing. Narratives tell stories and that is what we want children to learn to do themselves in this workshop. Most narrative writing is built around a story structure that includes five core components: character, setting, plot, movement through time, and change (Calkins, 2001). All children who listen to and eventually independently read narrative picture books should develop an understanding of these elements. In the very early grades (K–1), understanding character and setting is sufficient. Plot should be explained in the middle to later part of first grade. By second grade all of the elements should be thoroughly explained. The box below lists each of these key elements, along with a brief definition.

CHARACTERS — The people in the story

SETTING — Where and when the story takes place. A story often includes a broad setting—for example, a town—and, nested within it, other smaller settings, such as a school or a house.

PLOT — What the story is about. Children grasp this concept in terms of the beginning, middle, and end.

MOVEMENT THROUGH TIME — All stories start at one point in time and finish at a later point.

CHANGE — Change can be simple or complex, but there is always some kind of change in a story, such as changes in a character's feelings or opinions, or a change that signifies growth or resolution.

Although we start our reading workshop with a study of the overall genre of narrative, we next focus in on a specific kind of narrative—the personal narrative. Personal narratives are generally true stories told by the writer in first-person narrative. Because we will be asking children to do personal narrative writing, it is very helpful to read aloud at least one excellent personal narrative as part of the reading workshop.

Choosing authors and text carefully is a skill that takes time and experience to develop. To help you, I included a list of recommended picture books on page 80; this list groups books according to how strong they are in a particular story element. Encourage children to bring in books from home that follow the "story" rules. And remember—if you are excited about a book, your students will get excited, too.

The two picture books I've used for the unit in this book are *The Other Side* by Jacqueline Woodson and *Thank You, Mr. Falker* by Patricia Polacco. The first is a fictitious narrative, based on real-life events; the second is a personal narrative that relates a critical autobiographical experience from the author's childhood. Both are excellent examples of well-written, inviting narrative picture books that incorporate all the story elements. For the third week of the unit, I leave the choice of book to you but highly recommend *Shortcut* by Donald Crews or *Come On, Rain* by Karen Hesse.

I think you'll find that using narrative picture books is a great tool for helping to teach children to write their own personal narrative stories. Once young children have built a thorough understanding of story elements, they begin to feel more confident about writing their own stories. It really isn't very difficult for children to write stories that are based on their own lives. After all, isn't that what five-, six-, and seven-year-olds know the most about?

Focusing on Writing Key Story Elements

By the end of the reading workshop, children will have developed a genuine understanding not only of narrative structure but also of how stories grow from real lives. They are ready to launch into writing stories from their own lives. These next few weeks, when we delve into writing workshop, are an exciting time. They are the heart of the unit, and you'll quickly see why.

Taking Time to Get It Right

What is a writing workshop anyway? I like to describe it to my students in these simple terms: A workshop is a time when you keep working on something. I assure them that their pieces won't get completed the first day or even the first week. It comforts children to have this explained up front. They don't feel pressured to rush through a project. In fact, it's critical for even these very young children to realize that writing is an ongoing process. You need to help them realize that it's more important to get a piece of writing done right in a longer period of time than to finish quickly and incorrectly. You want them to spend time writing, making changes, rereading, and asking questions before they complete a piece (Graves, 1994). So when you launch your writing workshop at the beginning of the year, be sure to set up writing tasks that require many sittings.

A building block of the approach I present in this unit is the use of stretching strategies. This ensures that children don't just dash off a paragraph and consider it a complete piece of writing. We start from a story plan that they generate. The story plan has four major components: promise sentence (introduction); wondering part (where the tension is built); hot spot (story's climax, tension resolved); and closing (the end, where the pieces are tied up). The promise sentence is usually just that, a single sentence, but the other three parts need to be elaborated and stretched. Over the course of three weeks we employ three stretching strategies—describing the scene, explaining the characters' thoughts and feelings, and adding dialogue—to fully flesh out each story part.

Teacher Modeling Is Key

You'll notice that a strong teacher-modeling component guides the instruction during these four weeks of writing workshop. I strongly believe that children not only learn better from clear examples but they enjoy hearing you tell your stories. It inspires them in indescribable ways. You are a real live author sitting in front of them and you are showing them how it's done. In fact, most literacy experts, including Lucy Calkins (2001), agree that modeling your own writing in front of children is the most powerful strategy you can use to help them become good writers.

Modeling is also an ideal way to give struggling writers an entry into the writing process. If coming up with thoughts and ideas for their own pieces is too challenging, children can always go to your piece and use it as a starting point.

I realize that it is sometimes intimidating for teachers to write in front of their class. But try not to let a little discomfort get in your way. It helps to remember who your audience is—young children. They will love whatever you write! And don't underestimate how strongly your message will get across to your students while you show them what to do in your own work.

Role of the Story Elements

Upon reading through these writing workshop lessons, it may strike you that there's no specific instruction aimed at getting children to include the five story elements in their own stories. As you already know, before children get the opportunity to start writing their own pieces, the reading workshop immerses them in text that has good clear examples of all the story elements. They now have a strong understanding of these elements and should be able to identify them in text and discuss them. So why do we not ask children to specifically include these elements in their own writing?

I strongly believe in encouraging young writers to be risk takers. We want children to be creative writers who don't feel inhibited to try lots of new things. We hope that they will be excited about writing and jump right into their stories. At their stage of development, however, these young children are just discovering themselves as writers. Striking the right balance that allows them to flourish can be tricky. I have found that imposing too many rules on them—like expecting perfect spelling or excellent handwriting—can hold them back from the creative process.

This philosophy applies to the idea of explicitly demanding the use of story elements in their writing. Asking young children to set up their stories with all of the story elements before they write can be an overwhelming and stifling task. Instead, I have found that focusing on having children write a good story almost always results in a kind of organic success: Good stories wind up having all of the elements. The story elements fall into place as children progress through the writing process.

And, after the direct instruction during the reading workshop, they are indeed able to search out and identify the elements by name in their own writing. I ask them to do this only at the end of the unit, however. On our final day of the writing workshop, we use a checklist for story elements (page 79). After publication, children read one another's pieces and fill out this checklist. It is a great way for children to share their work and to give one another feedback.

One last comment about the story elements: You'll notice "Readers Make Good Writers" sidebars running throughout many of these lessons. These sidebars link the lesson at hand to the specific elements that are most relevant to that lesson. The boxes also point out how those elements are treated in the two model books, *The Other Side* and *Thank You, Mr. Falker*.

Revising, Editing, and Publishing

These lessons take children through the end of the writing-process journey for these personal narrative stories. During these final two weeks, you'll show them how to revise, edit, and finally publish their stories for sharing with the world. Revising means checking for content gaps, clarifying confusions, filling in missing words, and so on. Editing means correcting the mechanics—punctuation, capitalization, and spelling. Throughout both stages, I provide a few charts and reproducible checklists so that children can work independently to polish their work.

After revising and editing their work and having it approved by you, children enter the final publishing week. They copy over their stories as neatly as possible, illustrate them, and add covers. When the week is out, children have a genuine published product—a real story to share with peers and family. It's hard to know who feels prouder at this point, you or they!

With this book as your guide, I believe you will find that getting started and maintaining a successful writing workshop in your classroom is quite easy. It is truly a rewarding, joyful experience to watch young children blossom into writers. Good luck!

Weeks 1 to 3

Reading Workshop

The first step in teaching children to write narratives is to give them a strong understanding of what makes a story a story. We will do this during the first phase of the unit in a three-week reading workshop. For these initial three weeks we will immerse the class in story reading and in instruction about story elements.

In the first set of lessons, we use an excellent fictional narrative picture book, *The Other Side*, as the basis of instruction. Because we will be asking children to write personal narratives—stories of real experiences in their own lives—we focus the next set of lessons on an engaging personal narrative, *Thank You, Mr. Falker*. Finally, we repeat all story-element lessons with a third book, another personal narrative that you select. By the end of these three weeks, children will have become extremely familiar and comfortable with the structure of narrative writing.

Planning Calendar

Unit Week 1: Week of ____

Monday	Tuesday	Wednesday	Thursday	Friday
Lesson 1: **Identifying Narrative Books**	*Lesson 2:* **Learning Story Elements: Character**	*Lesson 3:* **Learning Story Elements: Setting**	*Lesson 4:* **Learning Story Elements: Plot**	*Lesson 5:* **Learning Story Elements: Movement Through Time**
• Define narrative writing • Identify narrative books • Look for good examples of narrative books • Set up a story basket	• Discuss: "What makes a story a story?" • Introduce the concept of story elements • Focus on the first story element: character • Read the narrative picture book, *The Other Side* • Make a character web • Start charting story elements	• Review the concept of story elements • Introduce the second story element: setting • Reread *The Other Side* • Continue charting story elements • Create umbrella graphic organizer for setting	• Review the concept of story elements • Introduce the third story element: plot • Continue charting story elements • Retell story: beginning, middle, and end	• Introduce the fourth story element: movement through time (time passing) • Reread *The Other Side*, with a focus on how time passes • Continue charting story elements

Planning Calendar

Unit Week 2: Week of _____

Monday	Tuesday	Wednesday	Thursday	Friday
Lesson 1: **Learning Story Elements: Change**	*Lesson 2:* **Focusing on Personal Narrative Books**	*Lesson 3:* **Learning Story Elements: Character**	*Lesson 4:* **Learning Story Elements: Setting**	*Lesson 5:* **Learning Story Elements: Plot**
• Review both the story chart for *The Other Side* and the story-elements chart • Introduce the fifth story element: change • Continue charting story elements	• Define personal narrative writing • Read aloud the personal narrative book, *Thank You, Mr. Falker,* by Patricia Polacco	• Repeat Lesson 1/2*: Focus on story element of character, using *Thank You, Mr. Falker*	• Repeat Lesson 1/3: Focus on story element of setting, using *Thank You, Mr. Falker*	• Repeat Lesson 1/4: Focus on story element of plot, using *Thank You, Mr. Falker*
		* Lesson 1/2 = Week 1/Lesson 2		

Planning Calendar

Unit Week 3: Week of _____

Monday	Tuesday	Wednesday	Thursday	Friday
Lesson 1: **Learning Story Elements: Movement Through Time**	*Lesson 2:* **Learning Story Elements: Change**	*Lesson 3:* **Learning Story Elements: Character and Setting**	*Lesson 4:* **Learning Story Elements: Plot and Movement Through Time**	*Lesson 5:* **Learning Story Elements: Change**
• Repeat Lesson 1/5: Focus on story element of movement through time, using *Thank You, Mr. Falker*	• Repeat Lesson 2/1: Focus on story element of change, using *Thank You, Mr. Falker*	• Repeat and combine in abbreviated form Lessons 1/2 and 1/3: Focus on story elements of character and setting, using a Tomie dePaola personal narrative or other favorite personal narrative book	• Repeat and combine in abbreviated form Lessons 1/4 and 1/5: Focus on story elements of plot and movement through time, using a Tomie dePaola personal narrative or other favorite personal narrative book	• Repeat Lesson 2/1: Focus on story element of change, using a Tomie dePaola personal narrative or other favorite personal narrative book

Identifying Narrative Books

Lesson Overview

This first lesson starts an ongoing conversation with children about the nature of **narrative writing** and how it is different from informational, expository writing. Together, you and your students will search for narrative books in your classroom and set up an unlabeled basket for gathering the storybooks. It's important to give children a chance to find the books themselves.

The tone of this lesson should be informal and fun. Children are exploring and actively learning. Encourage a good deal of classroom discussion as well as independent book time.

Although you do not address the five story elements explicitly in this lesson, the foundation is laid here for all subsequent reading workshop lessons. For now, simple exposure to the nature of narrative stories is important for these young writers.

Sample Lesson Dialogue and Instruction

Teacher: You all know a lot about reading. We have lots of different kinds of books in our library. Can you name some of the kinds of books you know? [*You will receive different answers depending on the grade level you teach.*]

Cassi: Fiction, nonfiction, picture books, chapter books.

Teacher: Yes, those are some books we know. How is a picture book different from a chapter book?

Jack: Chapter books are longer.

Julia: Chapter books don't always have pictures.

Teacher: Great. Now let's look at two different picture books. [*Hold up two books that are already familiar to students. For example, for the storybook, you could present* Owl Moon *by Jane Yolen or* Fireflies *by Julie Brinckloe; for the expository model, you might use any Gail Gibbons book, like* Check It Out!, Emergency!, *or* The Moon Book.] Who can tell me how these books are different?

Cassi: The first book tells a story. The second book tells a lot of facts.

Teacher: Yes, that's the most important way that they are different. When a book tells a story, it is called a *narrative* book. Can someone tell me what a story has that's different from a fact book? *[Children might offer comments such as, "A story has a beginning, a middle, and an end," or "People talk to each other in a story." For now, accept any appropriate characteristics without labeling or identifying them.]*

Teacher: Excellent. Soon we're going to learn even more about what makes a story a story. But right now, can you find some other narratives you have seen in the classroom?

Pair up children to conduct a quick search for narrative books. Then together hold up each choice, examine it with the class, and determine if the book should belong in a new basket that you will be adding to your classroom library. Do not label the basket yet. Some children may select books that don't belong. That's okay. Ruling out the ones that are not stories will help children better understand why the books that really are narratives should stay. Provide time for children to gather books and place them in the basket.

Teacher: We've found a lot of books to add to our new basket. Now you will know exactly where to find a narrative book. Tonight you might find some at home to bring in and add to our classroom basket, too.

End the lesson by giving children further opportunity to browse through these books.

Week 1/Lesson 2

Learning Story Elements: Character

Lesson Overview

At the start of this lesson, conduct a quick review of the concept of narratives and label the new book basket "Storybooks." Next, introduce the model narrative picture book *The Other Side* by Jacqueline Woodson. This book will be the basis for this and the next four lessons. It is the story of a young African-American girl who makes friends one summer with the white girl who lives on the other side of the fence. Introduce the term *story elements* and focus on the element of **character**.

In this lesson, you will also start two classroom charts: one listing story elements with brief definitions, and the second depicting the story elements specifically for *The Other Side*, using graphic organizers. Consider each chart as evolving; you will add the appropriate element during each reading workshop lesson until the charts are complete on the final day. (See page 26 for completed charts.) For this lesson, the graphic organizer is a character web. After reading aloud *The Other Side*, create a character web for major characters then assign children to make their own character webs.

Sample Lesson Dialogue and Instruction

Teacher: Yesterday we talked about narratives. Who can remind us what a narrative is?

Zach: Something that tells a story.

Teacher: Yes. We even made a new basket for our library that we filled with books we believe are stories. Let's label this basket "Storybooks." [*Use a marker and poster paper to label the basket.*] Today we are going to take a closer look at one specific narrative story. It's a book called *The Other Side.* [*Show the book to the class.*] Before I read this book, I want you to think again about what makes a story a story. What do you expect to see in this book that lets you know it is a story?

Ellen: There is a character on the cover.

Teacher: Yes, this book is about a little girl. Do you expect to see other characters?

Elijah: Yes, maybe her family or friends.

Teacher: So there might be a few characters in this book. You have just told me the first ingredient for a story—*characters*.

On a chart write "What Makes a Story a Story" and list *characters* as the first element. Next to the word *characters*, write the simple definition, "the people in the story."

Teacher: Writing a narrative story is like cooking. There are certain ingredients you need to have in order for the story to really be a story. They're all necessary. If you made chocolate chip cookies without all of the key ingredients, like the chips, you wouldn't have

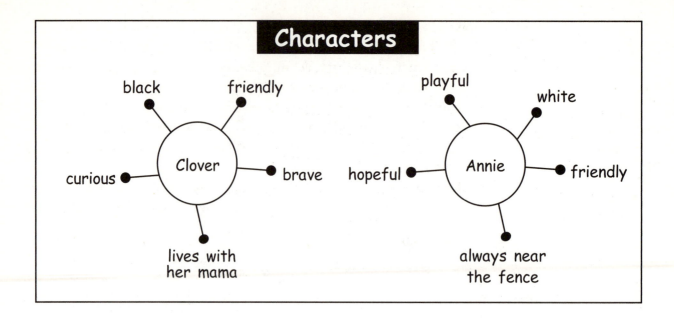

Characters

Clover
- black
- friendly
- curious
- brave
- lives with her mama

Annie
- playful
- white
- hopeful
- friendly
- always near the fence

chocolate chip cookies. So character is the first ingredient—or *element*—we will look at. The word *element* is a grown-up word for each ingredient of a story.

Read *The Other Side* to children. Make certain as you go along that they understand the story's big idea, but don't spend more than a minute on that. Today the focus is on characters, not plot.

Teacher: It feels like we all understand this story. Let's talk about the characters. Who did we meet in the book?

Katie: A little girl named Clover and a little girl named Annie.

Teacher: Right, and because the book is mostly about Clover, she is called the *main character*. That means the story is mainly about her. Did we meet any other characters in the book?

Gabriel: Yes, there were other friends and Clover's mama.

Once children have named the major characters, work with them to make a character web for each character, displaying his or her personal traits. (This is the beginning of the second chart. Label the chart "The Other Side," and be sure to leave enough room to fit the other story elements that you'll be covering in the next few lessons. See above for a completed set of sample character webs.)

To help young children grasp the concept of traits, you might discuss them as things that are part of a person's personality or body. For example, you could ask the class to comment on something about the way you look. They might come up with "dark eyes" or "brown hair." These are "outside" traits—things you know about a person just by looking at them. Then encourage children to name some things they know about you that they can't tell just by looking at you—"inside" traits. They might say things like "loves cats" or "is friendly." Their evidence for these observations might be something like, "Well, we know you have a cat so you must love cats. You have a lot of friends so you are a friendly person."

For homework or class follow-up work, have children make character webs of themselves. Remind them to include both inside and outside traits.

Week 1/Lesson 3

Learning Story Elements: Setting

Lesson Overview

In this lesson, continue the conversation begun the previous day about story elements. First, review the concept of elements with the class and check that children remember and understand the first element, character. Using the same picture book, *The Other Side*, shift the focus to the element of **setting**. There are several layers to this element—both the big-picture setting (for this book, it's a Southern town) as well as the smaller settings, or scenes. Reread the book. On the chart labeled "The Other Side," create an umbrella web for all the different settings. Add *setting* and its simple definition to the chart "What Makes a Story a Story." Conclude the lesson by having student partners prepare their own setting webs.

Sample Lesson Dialogue and Instruction

Before beginning this lesson, set up reading partners. Children can work with their partners for the remainder of this three-week reading workshop, or you may switch partners after the first two weeks. Depending on their reading levels, partners can choose books daily or stay with a book for a few days.

Teacher: Yesterday we read *The Other Side* and we talked about story elements. Remember that a story element is an ingredient in a story; it makes a story a story. Who

	remembers the story element we discussed yesterday? *[Point to chart.]*
Ian:	Characters.
Teacher:	Exactly. Today we will add to our list of story elements and see what else makes a story a story. Let's think about where this story takes place. Does anyone know what we call that? *[Provide time for children to respond; if they cannot come up with the term, offer the following explanation.]* This element is called the *setting*. It is a name for exactly what I said—where the story takes place. So, what is the setting of *The Other Side*?
Charlie:	In a town.
Jarred:	In a house.
Lucy:	In a yard.
Teacher:	It sounds like there might be more than one setting for *The Other Side*. We can find out by reading the book again. But first I'm going to show you a web that will help us get organized. *[Draw a picture of an umbrella on the chart for* The Other Side.*]* We will use each of these points on the umbrella for the different settings of the story. Let's start by deciding what should go inside the big part of the umbrella. Where is the big place in which the whole story takes place? Can we agree on one big place?
Avery:	They are in her town for the whole story but they visit different places in her town.
Teacher:	That is true. Is the town somewhere specific, somewhere that adds to the meaning of the story?
Jordan:	It's in the South, where people who were different weren't allowed to play together.
Teacher:	That's really important information to the story. *[In the top part of the umbrella write "Southern town."]* Now let's look at the points on this umbrella. They are for the setting changes, or scenes. A good analogy for setting changes in a book is to think about movies. Every time the story moves from one place to another in a movie, we see a new scene. So let's see how many different scenes there are in our book.

Read the story again. Encourage children to interrupt you to point out the scene changes; write the different settings under each point of the umbrella. A completed sample setting web follows:

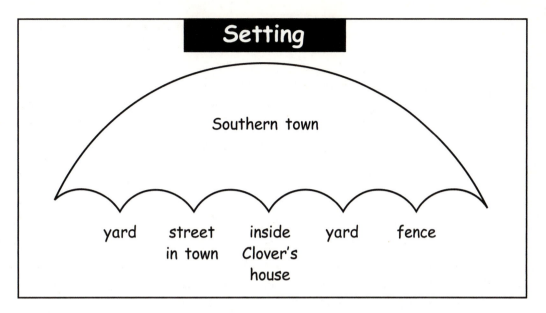

Setting

Southern town

yard | street in town | inside Clover's house | yard | fence

Teacher: So now we know the second ingredient, or element, you need to have to make a story. What is it?

Georgie: A setting.

Teacher: Great. Let's add it to our chart. *[On the chart "What Makes a Story a Story," list the term* setting *under* character *along with its brief definition, "where the story takes place."]* Now I'd like you to sit with your reading partner to discuss the setting of the narrative book you are currently reading. Make sure to talk about the different scenes in the book.

To conclude this lesson, have each set of partners make an umbrella web to share with the class.

Week 1/Lesson 4

Learning Story Elements: Plot

Lesson Overview

In this lesson, continue your class discussion about story elements. Begin by reviewing the concept of elements to make sure that children remember and understand the first two elements. Using *The Other Side*, shift the focus to the element of **plot**, or what happens in the story. Because even young children usually have at least a basic sense of beginning, middle, and end, plot is usually a fairly easy

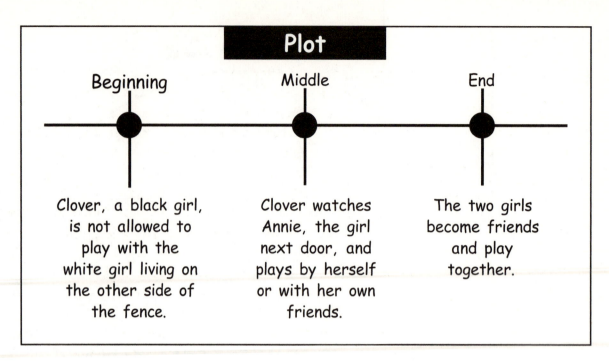

Plot

Beginning	Middle	End
Clover, a black girl, is not allowed to play with the white girl living on the other side of the fence.	Clover watches Annie, the girl next door, and plays by herself or with her own friends.	The two girls become friends and play together.

concept for them to grasp. Draw a plotline, with appropriate events provided by children, on the chart "The Other Side." Add *plot* and its simple definition to the classroom chart "What Makes a Story a Story." Conclude the lesson by having student partners draw their own plotlines.

Sample Lesson Dialogue and Instruction

Begin this lesson by reviewing the two story elements you have discussed during the previous two lessons. Remind children that a story must have both these elements to be considered a story.

Teacher: Today we're going to take a look at the next story element. This third element is called *plot*. Does anyone know what the plot of a story is?

Avery: Yes, it's what the story is about.

Teacher: That's exactly what the plot is. It's what happens in the story. Here's an easy way to help you remember what the plot is—think about the beginning, middle, and end of the story. Today let's do that with the book we've been reading together, *The Other Side*. [*If you feel that your class could benefit from a third reading, you may choose to read the book again. However, by this point most children should have a good enough understanding of the text to be able to retell the plot without hearing the story again.*]

Teacher:	*[Draw a plotline (see completed example on page 20) on the chart "The Other Side."]* Who can tell me what happened at the beginning of the story?
Hannah:	A little black girl who lives in the South isn't allowed to play with her next-door neighbor because she is white.
Teacher:	Great! You told me just enough to know what's important but you didn't tell me everything that happened in the first few pages of the book. Let's write that sentence on the chart. *[Write this sentence on the plotline.]*
Teacher:	What about the middle of the story?
Paul:	Well, the little girl Clover keeps watching Annie and does things during the summer alone or with her other friends.
Teacher:	Yes, the middle of the book is when we get to know how Clover spends her time. *[Write this on the plotline.]* How about the end?
Anna:	At the end of the story the girls all play together and they hope the fence gets taken down.
Teacher:	Okay, so at the end we see that things are changing in Clover's and Annie's lives. *[Write a sentence that describes the end on the plotline.]*
Teacher:	So now we know the third ingredient, or element, you need to have to make a story. What is it?
Ian:	A plot.
Teacher:	Great. Let's add it to our chart. *[On the chart "What Makes a Story a Story," list the term* plot *along with the definition, "what the story is about."]* Now I'd like you to sit with your reading partner to discuss the plot of the narrative book you are currently reading. Make sure to specially look out for what happens in the beginning, the middle, and the end of the book.

To conclude this lesson, have each set of partners make a plotline to share with the class.

Learning Story Elements: Movement Through Time

Lesson Overview

In this and the next lesson, we examine two story elements that are more challenging for young children to define. They are both abstract ideas that cannot be easily proven with concrete examples from the text. Children will have to infer examples to show that they understand the meaning of these elements. We start in this lesson with **movement through time**. After giving children clues about how to look for time passing, reread *The Other Side*. Elicit class discussion about time and add an explanatory sentence to your story chart. Add *movement through time* and its simple definition to the story-elements chart "What Makes a Story a Story." Conclude the lesson by having student partners search for and describe time passing in their independent reading books.

Sample Lesson Dialogue and Instruction

Teacher: We have already identified three of the five elements that make a story a story. Today we are going to look at the fourth one. In all stories there is some movement through time. We can define this as "time passing." If I tell you a story about my day at school and I start when I get here in the morning and I end when school lets out, how much time has passed in my story?

Chloe: One whole day.

Harriet: Seven hours.

Teacher: Both of those answers are correct. My story lasted for one whole school day, or seven hours. In all stories time passes. Let's read *The Other Side* one more time. As I read it, I want you to see if you can tell how much time has passed from the beginning to the end of the story.

As you read the book aloud, you may want to provide some clues for children. For instance, you might point out that the setting changes are a clue: Whenever the setting shifts, time has had to pass because the characters have moved from one place to another. You might

Movement Through Time

One Summer

Clues: "that summer. . ." "someplace in the middle of the summer. . ."

also point out that sometimes when Clover wakes up it's sunny and other times it's rainy. When a story spans more than one day, it is clear that time has passed.

Teacher: We noticed that time did move throughout the story. How much time would you say has passed in the book?

Willem: A few days passed because sometimes it was sunny and sometimes it was rainy.

Teacher: That is true. Can you think of a way of telling me about how many days has passed, or how much time has passed without using a number? Was it a season?

Monica: Yeah, it was the whole summer.

Teacher: I agree. The story takes place over one summer. Let's make sure to write how much time passed on our class chart about this book. *[On the chart "The Other Side," write a phrase or sentence that describes the passage of time, as well as clues from the story. See above.]* Now we know the fourth element you need to make a story. What is it?

Jordan: Moving through time.

Teacher: Yes, good. Let's add it to our story-elements chart. *[On the chart "What Makes a Story a Story," list the phrase* movement through time *along with the brief definition, "time passing."]* Now I'd like you to sit with your reading partner to discuss how time passes in the narrative book you are reading. See if you can identify how much time passes overall and if you can list some clues that tell you this.

To conclude this lesson, have each set of partners write one or two sentences about movement through time to share with the class.

Learning Story Elements: Change

Lesson Overview

In this lesson, we examine the final story element and probably the most challenging and abstract one for young readers—**change**. Although certain kinds of change (location or characters speaking, for instance) might seem obvious to children, the deeper kinds of change that typically involve the characters' thoughts or feelings are difficult to prove with concrete examples from the text. For example, in *The Other Side* the girls realize it's all right to play with each other and their attitudes change. Struggling learners may have trouble grasping and articulating this, but it's a critical idea to their understanding of the whole story. Although the element of change can be summed up in a sentence or two, it usually requires some class discussion to help children truly grasp it. (Note that in the book recommended for the second week of reading workshop, *Thank You, Mr. Falker*, the change is more obvious—the main character, Trish, learns to read. This is a great example of change that is easy to perceive but also profound.)

After class discussion, add an explanatory sentence about the change that takes place in the story to the story chart. Also, add *change* and its definition to the chart "What Makes a Story a Story." With this lesson, you and your class will have completed both charts. Conclude by having student partners search for and describe examples of change in their independent reading books.

Sample Lesson Dialogue and Instruction

Teacher: Today we've come to the last story element. First, let's look over both our charts to remind us what we know so far.

Review your two charts with the class, going over them point by point. Call on volunteers to help you explain each of the four elements listed on the story-elements chart. Refer to the other chart for an example of each element as you discuss it.

Teacher: Today's story element is called *change*. Can you name something that changed in the story?

Kathryn:	The girls were in her yard and then they were in her house.
Teacher:	That is one thing that changed. Sometimes in a story the setting might be the thing that changes. A lot of times it is a feeling or an attitude that the character has. Can you think of a way the characters changed in this book?
Maria:	Yes, the little girls did not play together in the beginning of the story but at the end they change their ideas and they play together.
Teacher:	You got it! The way the characters felt and thought changed as the story went on. In all the stories you read, there is going to be some sort of change going on. Let's finish our chart of story elements. *[On the chart "The Other Side," write a sentence that describes the major change that occurs in this story, as below.]*

Change

Clover and Annie become friends by the end of the story. They bring together black people and white people who had been separated.

Teacher:	So now we know the fifth element you need to make a story. What is it?
Emanuel:	A big change happens.
Teacher:	Yes, good. Let's add it to our story-elements chart. *[On the chart "What Makes a Story a Story," list the word change along with the definition, "the change that takes place in the story." See page 26 for completed charts.]*
Teacher:	You guys did a great job explaining all of the story elements in this book. Keep working on naming and explaining story elements when you read with your partners.

To conclude this lesson, have each set of partners write one or two sentences about change in their book to share with the class.

THE OTHER SIDE

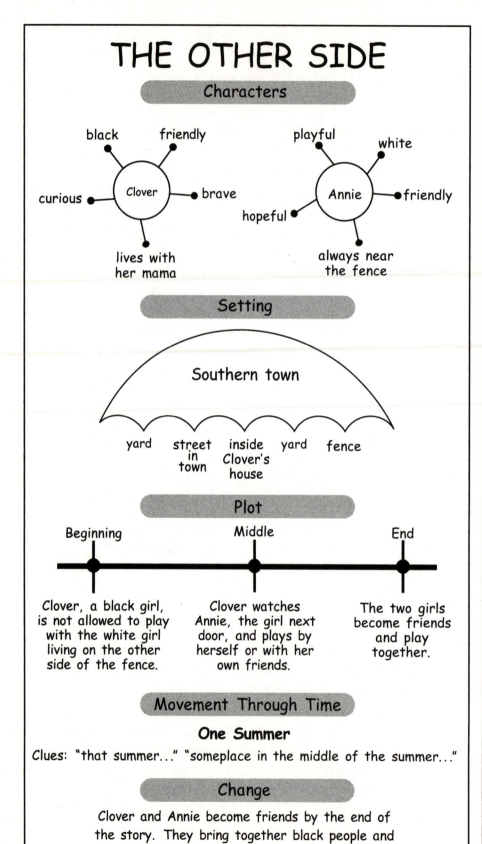

Characters

Clover
- black
- friendly
- curious
- brave
- lives with her mama

Annie
- playful
- white
- friendly
- hopeful
- always near the fence

Setting

Southern town

yard   street in town   inside Clover's house   yard   fence

Plot

Beginning	Middle	End
Clover, a black girl, is not allowed to play with the white girl living on the other side of the fence.	Clover watches Annie, the girl next door, and plays by herself or with her own friends.	The two girls become friends and play together.

Movement Through Time

One Summer

Clues: "that summer..." "someplace in the middle of the summer..."

Change

Clover and Annie become friends by the end of the story. They bring together black people and white people who had been separated.

What Makes a Story a Story
Five Story Elements: The Ingredients of a Story

Element 1: Character
The people in the story

Element 2: Setting
Where the story takes place

Element 3: Plot
What the story is about

Element 4: Movement Through Time
Time passing

Element 5: Change
The change that takes place in the story

Focusing on Personal Narrative Books

Lesson Overview

With their knowledge of story elements and the nature of narratives, children now have the foundation to learn about a special category of narrative—the **personal narrative**, or true story. Because personal narratives incorporate the same story elements, this lesson can serve as a review of those elements. But it also enables you to orient instruction increasingly toward the writing workshop weeks, in which children will create their own personal narrative stories.

It's worth noting that the sample dialogue provided here deliberately does not include the terms *fiction* and *nonfiction*. Technically, true stories are nonfiction in narrative format; made-up stories like *The Other Side*, even if based on real events, are narrative fiction. These distinctions are subtle and potentially confusing for young readers. Thus, the very first lesson taught children to distinguish between fact books (expository writing) and narrative books (stories). This lesson further differentiates narrative writing.

As is true of any instruction, your judgment of your own class's readiness and development is key. If your students are ready to think in terms of fiction and nonfiction narratives, then you may want to introduce the lesson within that framework.

Sample Lesson Dialogue and Instruction

Teacher: Now that we have a really good sense of the five elements that make a narrative story a story, we're going to take a close look at a special kind of narrative story. This type of story tells about something that really happened in a person's life. Another name for this type of story is *personal narrative.* [*Write this term on the chalkboard.*] It means a "true story from your life." We all have things that happen in our lives that can be made into stories. Can anyone think of an example?

Avery: Like the time I lost my cat and my sister and I searched everywhere and just when we almost gave up, we found him on my neighbor's roof.

Teacher: Yes, that sounds like it could make a great story. It's personal because it happened to you, and if you told it with a plot and characters and all the other elements we've studied, it would be a narrative. So that would be a personal narrative. Today we're going to read a new book. [*Hold up* Thank You, Mr. Falker.] It's a personal narrative book because it tells the story of what really happened in the life of the author when she was a little girl. As I read this book, I want you to think about all the story elements that we learned last week. They're all in here, I promise. Later, we'll make a chart for this book, just as we did for *The Other Side*. Let's start by looking at the cover. What do you see?

Julian: I see two characters on the cover.

Teacher: Yes, this book is about a young girl and her teacher.

Read the book aloud to children. For today, read it through just once without interruption so that children can take in the story. In subsequent lessons, you'll read it again, with an emphasis on each of the narrative elements.

Special Note

For the remainder of this week and for the next week, reading workshop lessons follow the same format that you used in Week 1/Lesson 2 through Week 2/Lesson 1. See the planning calendars on pages 11–12 for a recommended map of how the lessons flow. The first time you repeat the lessons, we suggest *Thank You, Mr. Falker*. You'll see references to its story elements, along with those from *The Other Side*, in the writing workshop lessons. For the third book, you might want to choose a Tomie dePaola personal narrative, such as *The Art Lesson* or *Nana Upstairs & Nana Downstairs*, or any other personal narrative that you consider a favorite.

Create a chart like the one for *The Other Side*, shown on page 26, for each book read. This repetition of reading workshop lessons will help children truly grasp the idea of story elements. At the end of three weeks your students should be experts in identifying and explaining story elements and you'll be ready to launch into the next exciting phase of this unit—the writing workshop.

Writing Workshop

I n this first week of the writing workshop, children take the essential steps to beginning their own stories. After weeks of reading and discussing narratives in reading workshop, children should have developed a firm grasp of the nature of narrative writing and its five building-block elements. They should also recognize the special characteristics of personal narratives. With that knowledge, children are now equipped to launch into writing their own stories.

Their first step is to find the idea that they want to write about. This is not as easy as it sounds for young children. There are three parts to this process. First, at the beginning of the year, have children generate their own lists of possible ideas. They can do this as homework, calling on family members to help them remember experiences. Next, in the workshop's first lesson, children select one big idea from this list. In the second

lesson, they home in further on their big idea by using a time line to map out the smaller events that are embedded in the larger one. By this point they have already made great progress toward starting their story—they are ready to write their first sentence, the *promise sentence*. From there, following your own model of how to make a story plan, children create an outline for their story. By the end of this week, they are ready to launch into the writing!

Note that, where appropriate in these lessons, you'll find explanations of how children's knowledge of specific story elements comes into play implicitly as they structure their own stories. Refer back to the introduction (page 4) for a discussion of how this approach works in our writing workshop.

Planning Calendar

Unit Week 4: Week of _____

Monday	Tuesday	Wednesday	Thursday	Friday
Lesson 1: **Generating Ideas: Finding the Story to Tell**	*Lesson 2:* **Making a Time Line to Focus on the Real Story**	*Lesson 3:* **Creating a Promise Sentence**	*Lesson 4:* **Making a Plan for the Story**	*Lesson 5:* **Reviewing the Parts of a Story**
• Remind students that in personal narratives, writers use ideas from their own lives to write about	• Discuss importance of choosing one part of a big story to focus on	• Read aloud promise sentences from several books	• Discuss importance of planning and outlining	• Review the key parts of the story identified in previous lesson
• Use completed sheet of writing ideas to model decision making	• Model creating time line of all the parts and events	• Discuss and define promise sentence: alerts the reader to the story's big idea	• Model telling aloud your whole story	• Students review promise sentences for their own stories
• Share students' take-home sheets	• Model choosing one part of time line for the story	• Model creating a promise sentence for your story	• Students note the sequential events of the story	• Students pair up and tell their stories to each other, starting with the promise sentences
• Pairs/small groups share stories from their sheets	• Students create their own time lines and select one idea	**Story elements tie-in: character, setting, plot, change**	• Make a plan for your story: list all the things that happen in the story	• Students make a plan for their stories
• Students choose a story they want to write about	**Story element tie-in: plot**		• Help students identify key parts of the story: promise sentence, wondering, hot spot, closing	**Story elements tie-in: character, setting, plot, change**
			Story elements tie-in: character, setting, plot, change	

Generating Ideas: Finding the Story to Tell

Lesson Overview

Getting ideas for writing is one of the hardest things for young writers to do. At the start of school it's helpful to send home a sheet on which children list ten ideas they have for things they might want to write about during the year. Tell children that the list will be kept in their own writing folder for them to refer to whenever necessary. Encourage them to list things they have done in their lives, such as learning to ride a bike. Suggest that they talk with their families to help them remember specific experiences.

Model ahead of time the format for listing ideas—that is, giving each idea a name. This way, when it's time to choose a story to write about, children already have a title and can call it by its name. For example, instead of listing "riding a bike," children can write, "When I learned how to ride a bike." (See page 32 for two examples of children's lists.)

This lesson, which marks the start of the writing workshop phase of this unit, is the first opportunity for children to put their lists to use. It works in tandem with the next lesson. On this first day, we help children decide which of their ideas they would like to write about. On the next day, we focus further on that idea and tease out the true story waiting to be told.

Sample Lesson Dialogue and Instruction

Have ready your own model sheet of writing ideas, filled out ahead of time with ten personal experiences that you might want to write about.

Teacher:	Today is an exciting day. We're going to start the next part of our personal narrative unit. We're going to begin the writing part. This week and for the next few weeks you're going to write your own personal narratives, just like those we've been reading. To get going, I want you to look over your lists of story ideas and think about how you might choose one idea for your story.
Julian:	I have ten ideas on my list.

Writing   *Ian*

we will be writing personal narrative stories for the next few weeks. Practice telling stories at home. Name each story you tell.

example: Taking the boat to Capri

1. When I Went to a bug zoo.
2. When I Went fishing.
3. Going to chack E. cheese.
4. Going to buggaboo Steak house.
5. Gardening With my Grand Pa.
6. What I want for christmas.
7. where I want to go on my next vacation;
8. Learning How to play the violin.

Writing   *Avery*

we will be writing personal narrative stories for the next few weeks. Practice telling stories at home. Name each story you tell.

example: Taking the boat to Capri

1. Riding a horse
2.
3. My Pets
4. Where I live
5. A day in Central Park
6. HoW I got hit with a baseball bat
7. About My grandma
8. About Portugal

Teacher: That's great. I know a lot of you have a lot of ideas. Me, too. I filled out my whole sheet. So first let's look at my list. [*Hold up your model sheet of ideas and point to a few items as you discuss them with the class. Think aloud to demonstrate your decision-making process.*] I think I have some great ideas. I'd love to write about the day I first got my cat, Oscar. I'd also love to write about my nephew's first-birthday party. And of course I could write about the year I taught first grade. But today the story that I feel that I have the most to talk about is my trip to Italy. It was the best trip I've ever taken and I have such great memories from that trip. It also happened just a few months ago, so the ideas are still fresh in my head. That's the story I want to write! Now it's time for *you* to share some of your ideas with us. [*Have children get out their own sheets. Hold a brief class discussion during which volunteers share their lists.*]

Set up small groups of three or four children and encourage them to share their story ideas, experimenting by telling their stories aloud for their peers. Help them choose the story they like best and would like to write about for this unit.

Making a Time Line to Focus on the Real Story

Readers Make Good Writers

Story element: *plot*

This lesson encourages children to call on their knowledge of the story element *plot* as they map out their time lines and choose the one big event that contains material that is potentially rich and interesting enough to become the basis of an original story. Children need to realize that too many events covered in one short narrative would be overwhelming to the reader; too few would be boring.

In *The Other Side*, for example, the author chose not to focus on the big events of the civil rights movement; instead she selected one small but important event embedded within that large movement.

Lesson Overview

In this lesson, children take another big step toward generating their own personal narrative. They take the one idea that they have already selected from their overall list and tease out the smaller events included in the larger idea. Following your model, they map the events on a bulleted time line. Afterward, they select the most interesting event—the one they can stretch into a real story. Just like that, children have the basis for the personal narrative that they will elaborate into a true story over the next few weeks.

Sample Lesson Dialogue and Instruction

Teacher: Remember that yesterday I looked at my list of ideas and decided to write about my trip to Italy. This is a great subject for me and I have so many things I could say about it but if I put them all in, my story would be too long and confusing and even boring. So I'm not going to write all about my trip. Instead, I'm going to pick one small part of my trip and tell you just that one small story. To do that, I'm going to use a special organizer called a *time line*. Writers often do this to help find the real story they want to tell. [*On a posterboard or transparency, draw a time line with five bullets.*] Can anyone describe what this time line does?

Avery: It looks like it lists all the things that happened on your trip.

Teacher: Yes! It helps you remember the things you did. Each dot represents a different part of my trip. [*Jot down events along the time line. Talk through each idea as you write it. A sample completed time line is below.*]

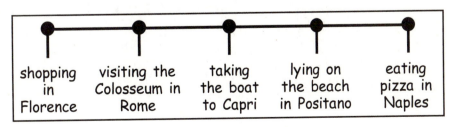

shopping in Florence | visiting the Colosseum in Rome | taking the boat to Capri | lying on the beach in Positano | eating pizza in Naples

Teacher: Wow, I did a lot of things in Italy. It looks like I could turn this time line into an all-about-Italy book, doesn't it? But I don't want to make an all-about book today. Today I'm making a personal narrative about one small story. So now I'm going to choose the one part of my time line that I want to turn into a story. What can I do to help me decide which part to turn into a story?

Leo: Think of the part you liked the best.

Justine: Think of the part you have the most to say about.

Go back over each event on the time line, thinking aloud as you remember the things that happened at each point. Some events may not be as interesting or rich in detail as others. Choose the one you can really stretch out.

Teacher: It seems like "taking the boat to Capri" is the part I have the most to say about. That's the idea I'm going to turn into a narrative. This is what I want you to try today. Yesterday you picked a big idea that you want to write about. Now you need to make your own time line of that topic and use your time line, just as I did, to choose the small part you want to turn into a personal narrative.

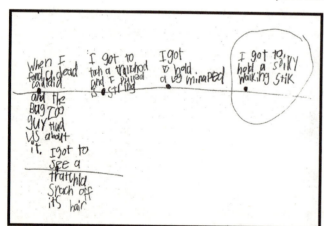

Have children work independently to make a time line of events and experiences for their chosen topic. Most will have stories that are big ideas, like a trip or hobby. These are ideal topics to break down on a time line. Afterward, ask them to select the most interesting event—the one part they want to write more about—and circle it. See below for two examples of children's time lines.

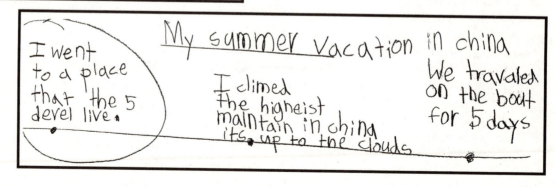

Creating a Promise Sentence

Lesson Overview

This is an exciting lesson because children start the actual writing of their stories. They begin with just one sentence, but that is a big step for novice writers. This first sentence, called a **promise sentence,** promises the reader what the big idea of the story will be. It also acts as a map for young writers, helping them to stay on track as they develop their stories. In this lesson, you provide two different models for children before they write their own promise sentences. First, read aloud a set of promise sentences from well-known narrative books. Next, demonstrate your own thinking as you come up with a promise sentence for your original story.

Sample Lesson Dialogue and Instruction

Teacher: Today we're going to start writing our personal narratives. Before we start, I want to share with you something good writers do at the very beginning of their books or stories. It's called a "promise sentence." Remember *Thank You, Mr. Falker*? The very first sentence is: "Trisha, the littlest girl in the family, grew up loving books." And remember, this turns out to be the story of a girl and her relationship with reading and books. So, the very first sentence gives us a very big clue. Here are some more promise sentences. After I read each one, I'll call on a volunteer to tell me what they think the book will be about.

Read aloud the first sentence of different narrative books. After each one, have a student predict what the story will be about. Here is a sampling of recommended books and their promise sentences:

- "My brother's a pain . . ." —from *The Pain and the Great One* by Judy Blume
- "We looked, we listened, we decided to take the shortcut home." —from *Shortcut* by Donald Crews
- "On a summer evening I looked up from dinner, through the open window to the backyard." —from *Fireflies* by Julie Brinckloe
- "It was late one winter night when Pa and I went owling." —from *Owl Moon* by Jane Yolen

Readers Make Good Writers

Story elements: *character, setting, plot, change*

It may be only a single sentence, but embodied in this first promise sentence is the writer's setup for the reader of what the entire story is about. In creating this sentence, our young writers call upon their knowledge of **character, setting,** and **plot.** In order to write a good promise sentence, they need to already have a good sense of their whole story: who is in the story, where it takes place, and what they plan to have happen in the story. All of this information probably will not be included in the one sentence, but it needs to be percolating in the writer's mind.

In *The Other Side*, the promise sentence lets the reader know both the setting—a town in the summer—as well as

(continued on page 36)

- "When Tommy was a little boy he had a grandmother and a great-grandmother." —from *Nana Upstairs & Nana Downstairs* by Tomie dePaola
- "In the night I woke up." —from *Salt Hands* by Jane Chelsea Aragon

(continued from page 35) an inkling of plot and change. The author tells us that the fence "seemed bigger" at the beginning of the summer, foreshadowing an event/change.

In *Thank You, Mr. Falker,* the promise sentence introduces the reader to the character of the grandpa and sets up the plot for readers, leaving them wondering what books have to do with honey.

Teacher: Let's think of a promise sentence as a promise the writer makes to the reader. In the first sentence, the author is promising you what this piece is going to be about. Whenever you start a new piece in writing, you need to have a promise sentence. You need to tell the reader what your story is going to be about from the very beginning. You're promising the reader that you are going to stick to the idea in the first sentence for the whole piece. Before you create your own promise sentence for your story, I'm going to show you how I make one for my own story. [*Display your time line.*] Remember this is the part I decided to write my personal narrative about. [*Point to the bullet that says "taking the boat to the island of Capri."*] What do I need at the very beginning of this piece?

Anna: A promise sentence.

Teacher: Yes, and today all I'm going to do is write the promise sentence for the story about taking the boat to Capri. Okay, let's see. What if I just say, "taking the boat to Capri"? Does that sound right?

Rose: No, that sounds more like a title.

Teacher: You're right. And I think I like the sound of "taking the boat to Capri" for my title. So maybe I already have my title. But I still need my promise sentence. When you write your promise sentence, make sure it sounds like the first sentence of a story and not like a title. You might need to say it out loud to hear what it sounds like and ask yourself if it sounds like a promise sentence or a title. [*If you feel children could use extra practice, say aloud a few sentences and a few phrases and challenge them to correctly identify each.*] Okay, so since my whole personal narrative is going to be about my boat trip to Capri with my husband, Scott, I think this might be a good promise sentence: *Scott and I took a boat from Positano to the island of Capri.* If you read this, would you think my story is going to be about Rome?

Charlie:	No.
Teacher:	Would you think it was going to be about pizza?
Charlie:	No.
Teacher:	What *do* you think this piece is going to be about?
Elijah:	It's going to be about what happened on the boat.
Teacher:	That's it. So, yes, there's my promise sentence. Today I want you to go back to your time line. Go back to the part of the time line you circled and start your story by creating your promise sentence. If it happens that your title comes out today that's fine, but I'm really looking for you to make your promise sentence. Your promise sentence is not only a way of telling the reader what the whole story will be about. It will also help you remember to stay on track and not write about things that don't fit into your story.

Have children work independently or in partners to create their promise sentences. Three sample promise sentences follow:

I was At a bug Zoo to hold a SPiKY walking stik.

I climed the higheist mahitain in china.

☺ Its fun to go on a Buzz lihtyear ride!

Making a Plan for the Story

Lesson Overview

In this lesson, children learn how to make a plan for a piece of writing, a step I highly recommend. In fact, making a plan for every story and piece of writing is mandatory all year long in my class. Planning is actually a kind of outlining—it allows children to identify the most important points in the story. As part of the planning process, encourage children to tell their stories out loud. Doing so helps young writers organize the parts into a whole. It also helps them think about what they want their story to sound like.

The process is, in a sense, circular: Children orally tell the story as fully as possible, and then they make a plan for the story by distilling and writing down only the key events and experiences. In subsequent weeks, they flesh out the story according to this plan and wind up with a full, written version of the story again.

This lesson also introduces children to the remainder of the key story structure terms that they will employ during the writing workshop. At the same time, it sets the stage for the stretching strategies they will use as they learn to write not simply skeletal, but well-developed, richly detailed narratives in the weeks to come.

Sample Lesson Dialogue and Instruction

Teacher:	We have been talking about starting to write personal narratives. Who can tell us what we know so far about what we must have to get started with our stories?
Alyse:	We need a promise sentence.
Teacher:	That's right. What is a promise sentence?
Chloe:	It's the first sentence of your piece that lets the reader know what you're going to be talking about.
Teacher:	Exactly. Now that we have our promise sentences we are ready to start the next part of our writing. We need to make a plan for our piece. A plan is like a list of the important points you need to tell in your story. One way to figure out what you want to say in your story is to tell the whole story out loud to someone else. Then you can think about it and figure out what is most important. So I'll start. I'm going to tell you my story about going on the boat to Capri.

Readers Make Good Writers

Story elements: *character, setting, plot, change*

Because the plan is the basis for the whole piece of writing, and all subsequent writing will stem from the plan, creating it calls upon the young writer's knowledge of most of the story elements. As they set up their plan, writers establish how their readers will meet the **characters**, recognize the **setting**, learn the **plot**, and probably discover the **change**. Writers need to incorporate all the key ideas for the story in their plan in order to follow it and stretch it out as they do their actual writing.

Tell your story orally to the class. As you do this, pay attention to two particular areas that make a good story. First, structure your story according to the basic framework of a narrative with a key opening sentence (promise sentence), building of tension (wondering part), climax (hot spot), and ending (closing). Second, strive to incorporate the kinds of details that make a story full and alive. Elaborate and enrich your story by describing the scene, explaining what you were thinking and feeling, and adding dialogue between yourself and others.

These two strategies will become the focal points of all the rest of the instruction in the writing workshop. In this lesson we provide direct instruction for only the first point, the narrative framework. For now children simply listen to your story, which will serve as a model of good, detailed storytelling. A sample story follows:

Scott and I took a boat from Positano to the island of Capri. We stood on the dock waiting for the boat to arrive. It was a clear, sunny day. We watched the waves of the ocean crashing against the shore.

I wondered what it would be like in Capri. I was so excited to lie on the beach and relax in the warm Italian sun. "Do you think the beaches in Capri will be nice?" I asked Scott. He shrugged his shoulders and stared out into the water. Then he answered, "We've certainly heard wonderful things about them!"

Just then the boat pulled in. We walked up the ramp and looked for a seat. The boat was pretty full but luckily we found two seats right near the window. The window was large and round. The sunlight shined through and bounced off the yellow walls of the boat. I couldn't wait to get to Capri. I realized how happy I was just to be on the boat with Scott. I reminded myself how lucky I was to be in this beautiful place with my favorite person. But still, I couldn't wait to get to Capri!

After what felt like hours, the captain finally announced that we were arriving. I got so excited I jumped out of my seat and ran to the front of the boat.

In the distance I saw it—Capri! It was large and green with hills rolling along the sides. The water surrounding the island was sparkling blue. The beaches looked beautiful. I knew I would love Capri.

I looked at Scott as we pulled into the dock and smiled. "We're here," I whispered. He smiled back and exclaimed, "I don't think you're going to be disappointed. It looks extraordinary!"

We walked out of the boat and down the ramp. We walked through the winding streets and went straight to the beach. The soft, warm sand slipped through our feet. "It's everything I pictured and even better!" I burst out to Scott. I was smiling from ear to ear. I knew we were going to have a great day on the island of Capri.

Teacher: Now that you have heard my story, I want you to watch how I plan for my piece.

Model how you create a plan for your story. Explain that you are not writing the whole story. Instead, you are focusing on just the few things that will help you remember what happened. As you write down the plan, ask children what they think should come next. Since they have just heard your story, they should remember the order of the main events. Here's a sample plan for the story:

- Scott and I waited for the boat to Capri.
- I wondered what it would be like on the island of Capri.
- We got on the boat to Capri.
- We arrived at the island.
- Scott and I went to the beach on Capri.

Teacher: Now that I have made my plan, I want us to think about which part of the story, which idea on the plan, is going to be the most exciting. Which idea do you think is the most important?

Philip: Maybe the part when you finally see Capri.

Teacher: Why do you think that part?

Philip: Because that's when we find out what we've been wondering about, when you are going to get there.

Teacher: Right. So that's the most important part of my story. We call that the "hot spot." It's the part of the piece where you discover what you have been wondering about. Let's write *hot spot* next to that part of the plan. [*Follow the same process for helping children to label each of these parts of the story: promise sentence, wondering part, and closing. (The sample story plan will be used as a classroom chart for ongoing reference.)*]

- Scott and I waited for the boat to Capri. **(promise sentence)**
- I wondered what it would be like on the island of Capri. **(wondering part)**
- We got on the boat to Capri. **(wondering part)**
- We arrived at the island. **(hot spot)**
- Scott and I went to the beach on Capri. **(closing)**

Teacher:	Let me ask you a question. Is there anything in my plan that wasn't in my story?
Julian:	No.
Teacher:	Did I say a lot more in my story?
Avery:	Yes.
Teacher:	Right. The plan just helps you remember what happened in the story. When I go to write my story I'll be stretching out each part of my plan and turning it into a longer piece. And so will you as you become real writers of personal narratives during the next few weeks. But first, you'll each make a plan for your story. And that is exactly what you'll do tomorrow.

Reviewing the Parts of a Story

Lesson Overview

This lesson picks right up from the direct instruction you provided in the previous lesson. After a brief review of the previous days' concepts, children work with their own promise sentences, telling their stories orally to a partner and writing down their story plans. This lesson acts as a springboard for children's actual writing of their personal narratives, which begins next week.

Sample Lesson Dialogue and Instruction

Teacher:	Today you are going to make a plan for your own story. First, let's review what a story plan is and let's go over the names of the four parts of the story that you need to remember. *[Facilitate a class discussion about your own story plan from the previous lesson and review these four concepts/terms:* promise sentence, wondering part, hot spot, closing.*]* Which part have you all written so far?

Promise Sentence: Georgie's dad told me she was going to my school.

Wondering Part:
. When I whas exsided about Georgie.
. when I met Georgie

Hot Spot: *. When I went to Georgie house for the first time
. when Georgie came to my house

Closing: . when She was in my class

W:\CRW\PersonalLines.Doc 9/28/01-rb

When I first got to the new apertment.

Promise Sentence: When I moved People came from next door

Wondering Part:
. the neigbors came to help unpack the heavy stuff!

Hot Spot: *. I ran arownd the hall dressed like a spy.

. I played awrond the boxes with my sisster

Closing: . I vached more and more stuff come in.

Elizabeth: Our promise sentences.

Teacher: That's right. So let's start with those. [*Have children get their promise sentences. Organize the class into partners.*] **Read over your promise sentence to remind yourself what your story is about. Then tell that story to a friend. Let your partner tell their story to you. After you have both told your whole story, you need to make a plan for your piece. Don't forget to label the parts of your plan, just the way I did for my plan yesterday.**

Circulate about the room as children tell their stories and write down their story plans. Help them as necessary.

Writing Workshop

This is the week in which the real work starts. It is a week full of energy, learning, and excitement. Children start to turn their story plans into real stories. The context for their writing this week is a limited but essential part of narratives—the tension-building section at the beginning of almost all stories. Readers wonder: What will happen? For young children, we call this, quite literally, the "wondering part." Within this section, children learn to apply each of the three major stretching strategies. With your sample story as a model, they learn the importance of describing a scene with details, explaining what their characters are feeling, and incorporating conversation and dialogue.

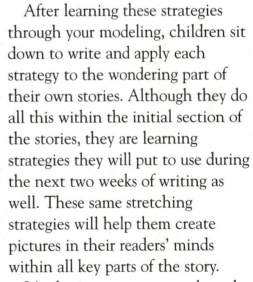

After learning these strategies through your modeling, children sit down to write and apply each strategy to the wondering part of their own stories. Although they do all this within the initial section of the stories, they are learning strategies they will put to use during the next two weeks of writing as well. These same stretching strategies will help them create pictures in their readers' minds within all key parts of the story.

It's also important as you launch into real story writing that children continue to think about what makes a good story. Always be ready to discuss and review with children all the things they have noticed about what good writers do in the read alouds you shared during weeks 1, 2, and 3. This should always be in the back of their minds so they use these strategies in their writing.

Planning Calendar

Unit Week 5: Week of _____

Monday	Tuesday	Wednesday	Thursday	Friday
Lesson 1: **Focusing on the Wondering Part of the Story**	*Lesson 2:* **Introducing the Stretching Strategies**	*Lesson 3:* **Using Stretching Strategies: Describing the Scene**	*Lesson 4:* **Using Stretching Strategies: Explaining What the Narrator/ Main Character Is Thinking and Feeling**	*Lesson 5:* **Using Stretching Strategies: Adding Dialogue**
• Review the concept of tension: leaving the reader wondering, not telling everything	• Explain the importance of stretching one's writing to help readers get a good picture of a story in their mind	• Review that writers use different strategies to help readers get a good picture of a story in their mind	• Discuss how explaining what the narrator or main character thinks and feels helps readers feel as if they are right there with the characters	• Discuss how making characters speak in conversation helps readers feel as if they are right there in the story
• Present a good example and a poor example of how stories can build tension	• Explain that writers use stretching strategies within each major story part	• Discuss how to use the "describing the scene" strategy within the wondering part of the story	• Model how to "explain what the narrator/main character is thinking and feeling"	• Model how to "add dialogue"
• Students evaluate these stories and explain their choices	• Model how to use stretching strategies within the wondering part of the story	• Students use this strategy to stretch the wondering part of their stories	• Students use this strategy to stretch the wondering part of their stories	• Students use this strategy to stretch the wondering part of their stories
Story elements tie-in: plot, change		**Story element tie-in: setting**	**Story element tie-in: character**	**Story element tie-in: character**

Using Picture Books to Teach Narrative Writing SCHOLASTIC TEACHING RESOURCES

Focusing on the Wondering Part of the Story

Readers Make Good Writers

Story elements: *plot, change*

In the wondering part of a story, where tension is deliberately created, two key story elements come into play—**plot** and **change**. It is here that writers start developing the real action of the story, setting up readers for the bigger things that are going to happen in the story. Thus, as writers create their story, they must have a sense of the big picture, of how the plot's events are going to build and unfold.

Writers' awareness of the story element of change is also critical here. It is in this beginning segment of the story that writers set up their readers to expect change, to anticipate the unexpected, and indeed to experience tension.

(continued on page 46)

Lesson Overview

In this lesson, children prepare further for launching into the heart of their story writing, which will take place during the latter three lessons this week. Today they learn in greater depth about the all-important story part that follows the promise sentence and leads up to the hot spot—the **wondering part**, where tension and suspense are built. After a class discussion, present children with two brief narratives—one that incorporates a well-written wondering part and another that lacks this part. In analyzing and evaluating what makes one a good example and the other a poor one, children are taking another key step toward understanding how to successfully structure their own stories.

Sample Lesson Dialogue and Instruction

Teacher: Last week we made story plans and wrote promise sentences for our personal narratives. This week we're going to get started on the real writing. But first we're going to learn more about the beginning part of the story. We already talked about this last week. Think back to our discussions. What's a smart thing you know that writers do when they write a good story?

Ian: They make a plot for their story.

Teacher: Yes, that's one important thing. And do you remember what writers do in the beginning of the plot? The part that comes right after the promise sentence?

Laura: I know! They keep you wondering.

Teacher: That's it. And how do authors keep you wondering?

Maria: They keep you wondering by making you think about what is going to happen. They don't tell you the whole story in the beginning.

Teacher: That's exactly what smart writers do when they write stories; they try to keep the reader wondering. In writers' language, this is called "building tension" or "creating suspense." Remember on our story plan *[point to display chart of the labeled story plan]* we call it the "wondering part." Today I'm going to

(continued from page 45)

In *The Other Side*, the tension is established in the first few pages. By introducing both the fence as a forbidden place to go and a young white girl who is always sitting on the fence, the author sets us up from the start to wonder: What is going to happen on that fence?

On the first page of *Thank You, Mr. Falker*, the main character, Trisha, reflects about learning how to read, and on the very next page we find out that she isn't reading like the rest of her peers. Will she learn to read? We are drawn in and wondering even this early in the story.

share with you two examples of stories. One example is not very good. It doesn't have a wondering part at all. The other is an example of a good story. It makes you wonder what's going to happen next. You have to figure out which one is good and be able to explain why.

Divide the class into partners or small groups. Read aloud, or write on a transparency or chalkboard, the following brief story examples.

One day I decided to get myself a cat. I walked into the shelter and found Oscar right away. He was perfect. Long brown hair, bright blue eyes, sweet and loving. I knew he was the cat for me. No one else wanted him. I took him home with me and he has lived with me ever since. He has his own cat bed. We are good friends now and I think we always will be.

One day I decided I wanted to learn how to ice skate. My friend was having an ice-skating party and I wanted to go. I wasn't sure my parents would agree. I thought of ways to ask them. It took three days. Each day at breakfast I gave a new reason I should be able to take lessons. Finally, my parents agreed! I took lessons and learning was worth all the falls I had. The party was so much fun.

After children have evaluated these stories, bring the class together to share their opinions. Guide the discussion so that children correctly identify the second story as a good example of building suspense and so that they are clear about what makes a good "wondering part."

Teacher: Now we all know that in a good story authors build suspense. They don't give everything away. This week, you are going to write stories that keep the reader wondering.

Introducing the Stretching Strategies

Lesson Overview

This lesson introduces children to the concept of using stretching strategies, which is central to all the writing that they will do during the rest of this week and during weeks 6 and 7. Through class discussion they come to realize that the wondering part of a story needs more than just a sentence or two. There is no wondering if a writer simply includes a skeletal point or two! With the importance of stretching out their writing established, children will observe how you flesh out your original story. This instruction sets the stage for the beginning of the real writing, which children will launch into the following day.

Sample Lesson Dialogue and Instruction

Teacher: Now we know a lot about the wondering part of a story. I want to go back to my own story today to write the wondering part. I'm going to start by looking at the wondering part on my story plan. [*Display the story plan from Week 4/Lesson 4 and point to the wondering parts.*]

- I imagined what it would be like on the island of Capri. **(wondering part)**
- We got on the boat to Capri. **(wondering part)**

Teacher: Okay, there it is—I've planned for a wondering part. I know I don't want to tell my readers right away what it was like getting to Capri. So do you think I can write exactly the words from my plan for my story?

Robbie: Yes, it makes sense.

Teacher: Well, it does make sense. So I'll write it next. [*On the board or a transparency, write those two story-plan sentences in paragraph format.*] But now I'm looking at it again. I'm asking myself whether these two sentences really build suspense. Let me ask *you* a question: Do you think that's all I need to say about what happens before I get to Capri?

Cassi:	No. I bet you have a lot more you could say!
Teacher:	You know, I agree. I'm not feeling much suspense at all from those two sentences. I need to turn this part into more than one or two sentences. In fact, we writers need to stretch out each part of our story and really try to make a picture in the reader's mind. We already know that from reading all our good picture books. But now the question is, *how* do I say more than just what I've got on my plan?
Katie:	I know. You need to add more details!
Teacher:	That's exactly right. But they can't just be any details. We're going to learn to add important information to each story part. We're going to do it using what we call "stretching strategies." Stretching strategies help us stretch out the story. Now watch as I stretch out these sentences into a story.

Model how you stretch out the wondering part of your story. (Note: For your convenience, the example below uses **boldface** for sentences that describe the scene, *italics* for those that explain the narrator's thoughts and feelings, and underlining for dialogue.)

Wondering Part in Sample Story

Scott and I took a boat from Positano to the island of Capri. We stood on the dock waiting for the boat to arrive. It was a clear, sunny day. We watched the waves of the ocean crashing against the shore.

I wondered what it would be like in Capri. I was so excited to lie on the beach and relax in the warm Italian sun. <u>"Do you think the beaches in Capri will be nice?" I asked Scott. He shrugged his shoulders and stared out into the water. Then he answered, "We've certainly heard wonderful things about them!"</u>

Just then the boat pulled in. We walked up the ramp and looked for a seat. The boat was pretty full but luckily we found two seats right near the window. The window was large and round. The sunlight shined through and bounced off the yellow walls of the boat. *I couldn't wait to get to Capri. I realized how happy I was just to be on the boat with Scott. I reminded myself how lucky I was to be in this beautiful place with my favorite person. But still I couldn't wait to get to Capri!* *

After you have written this whole wondering part, read it aloud for the class.

Teacher:	Are you wondering anything yet?
Wendy:	Yeah, I'm wondering how Capri was.
Greg:	I'm feeling curious.
Teacher:	Exactly. That's the point. I must have done it right because I got my readers to wonder. I didn't tell you right away that Capri was great. I'm making you wait to find out how it was. And I did that by stretching out this section. I'm building a picture in my readers' minds. Are you seeing it? Do you think I wrote enough about that part of the plan?
Class:	Yes.

* Note that in real classroom situations, the eventual written stories will wind up being similar—but not identical—to the original verbal stories that children generated during the planning phase (Week 4). However, for purposes of illustration, we're presenting the written story as a verbatim version of the original verbal story (as shown on page 39).

Using Stretching Strategies: Describing the Scene

Readers Make Good Writers

Story element: *setting*

The first stretching strategy, describing the scene, is intimately connected to the story element of **setting**.

As writers help their

(continued on page 50)

Lesson Overview

After a quick review of the role of stretching strategies and why they're important, this lesson focuses on one of those strategies as applied to one story part—describing the scene within the wondering part. It's important to model this strategy, and the other two in the next two days, in such depth and detail because children are launching into writing their own stories now. The more exposure they have to good writing, the more comfortable they will feel about trying to write. After you walk through the specific ways in which you stretched the wondering part of your story by describing the scene, invite children to get out their story plans and their promise sentences and to begin writing.

Sample Lesson Dialogue and Instruction

(continued from page 49) readers visualize where the story is taking place and provide descriptive details that flesh out the background, they are establishing the story's setting. Giving readers clues about the weather, colors, noise, smells, and other sensory things helps them feel as if they are in that place with the writer.

In *The Other Side*, the setting is clearly stated in the author's references to the fence, the town, the rain—all the things that Annie observes. Such details allow us, the readers, to grasp the story's environment and what is important about that environment.

In *Thank You, Mr. Falker*, we are introduced to the setting from the very beginning of the book. The description of the children at school, the classroom, and the words Trisha tries to read combine to help us create a picture in our minds of the background for the entire story.

Teacher: Today is a big day in our writing workshop. You're going to use your story plans and your promise sentences to begin your real writing. What's the part you'll be writing first?

Leo: The wondering part.

Teacher: Yes, that's the part you need to write first. And what's the important thing we discussed yesterday about what smart writers do in each part of their story?

Rose: They make a picture in the reader's mind.

Teacher: Absolutely! You want to make readers feel like they are right there with you. We do that by giving them lots of details, remember? And you already know that to give details, writers use stretching strategies. So today we're going to focus on one stretching strategy. Today we'll work on "describing the scene" in the wondering part of our stories. Let's look back at the wondering part of my story. *[Display transparency from yesterday's lesson or write this part on the board (see page 48).]* What are some ways I described the scene?

Jorge: You explained how it looked when you said, "It was a clear, sunny day."

Teacher: Exactly. I explained what it looked like around me. *[Underline this sentence and each subsequent sentence or phrase that you call attention to.]*

Jorge: And you talked about waves crashing! That really made me imagine the waves.

Teacher: Good. That's a part of the scene where I used the dramatic word *crashing* to give the feeling of the sound of the waves. *[Skip ahead to the paragraph that starts "Just then the boat pulled in." Point to it as you discuss it.]* Here's another place where I described the scene. Why didn't I just say we were sitting on the boat?

Liam: Because we wouldn't know how you got on the boat.

Teacher: Right. So watch how I let the reader know that I got on the boat without just saying, "Then we went on the boat." *[Point to the sentence, "We walked up the ramp and looked for a seat."]*

Teacher: Now do those words help make a better picture for you in your mind?

Ryan:	Yes, because now I know there was a ramp.
Teacher:	Yes, I made a better picture for you. *[Walk children through the rest of the paragraph that describes the scene, helping them see why each of the sentences or phrases paints a better picture for the reader.]*
Teacher:	Today I want you to begin writing your piece. Take out your papers that have your promise sentence on the top of the page and your story plans. *[See Week 4/ Lessons 3 and 5.]* Start with the first part of your plan and use everything you just learned about the "describing the scene" stretching strategy to turn that wondering part into a story that makes a good picture in the reader's mind.

Circulate about the room, supporting children as needed, as they work on writing the first part of their stories.

Readers Make Good Writers

Story element: *character*

The strategy of explaining the narrator's or main character's thinking and feeling presents a clear tie-in with the story element of **character**. By letting the reader into the mind of a story character, the writer is providing key

(continued on page 52)

Using Stretching Strategies: Explaining What the Narrator/Main Character Is Thinking and Feeling

Lesson Overview

In this lesson, children continue writing the wondering part of their story—stretching and fleshing it out from the few bullets they have outlined on their story plan. Here they learn more about the second stretching strategy, which builds in characters' thoughts and feelings. The lesson follows the same pattern as the previous lesson—first, children learn through teacher modeling and discussion of your original sample story. Afterward, children get out their own stories and elaborate further on the wondering part in their own writing.

Sample Lesson Dialogue and Instruction

(continued from page 51)
information about the character's personality and attitudes.

In *The Other Side,* we are let into Annie's thoughts and feelings through implication (the author tells us that through Annie's eyes "everything on the other side of that fence seemed far away") and directly (when the rain stopped, Annie "felt brave that day, she felt free").

In *Thank You, Mr. Falker,* a good deal of the story revolves around the feelings of the main character, Trisha, and her sadness and frustration about not being able to read. For example, when she starts first grade, "Trisha began to feel different, she began to feel dumb." Through these kinds of revelations, the author brings us right into Trisha's own world.

Teacher: Today you're going to continue working on turning your story plan into a real story. We still have more stretching work to do on the first part of the story, the wondering part, where you build suspense for the reader. Which stretching strategy did we use yesterday to make a picture in the reader's mind?

Carly: We described the scene.

Teacher: That's exactly right. Today we're going to learn how to explain what the narrator or main character is thinking and feeling. When we add these kinds of details, we make the story much more interesting for our readers. Now let's look again at the wondering part of my story. *[Display transparency from Week 5/Lesson 2 or write this part on the board (see page 48).]* What are some ways I made you feel like you saw what I saw and knew how I felt?

Jen: You explained how you felt where it says, "I wondered what it would be like."

Teacher: That's right! Right there in my story I let the reader in on what I was thinking and wondering about. *[Underline this sentence and each subsequent sentence or phrase that you call attention to.]* And what about the very next sentence? What do I do there?

Philip: You say you are excited. That means you're telling us how you're feeling.

Teacher: Good. That's where I'm explaining my feelings about what the beach will be like! *[Call attention to the sentence, "I couldn't wait to get to Capri" and to the following three sentences.]* Here's another place where I'm telling you my feelings. What do readers find out here?

Katie: That you think you're lucky!

James: That you're happy!

Teacher: Does knowing all that help make a better picture for you in your mind?

Molly: Yes, because otherwise we wouldn't know whether you liked what you were doing.

Teacher: I think you can see that knowing how a character or a person telling the story is feeling is really important.

It gives readers a much better sense of what is happening and what the story is about. Now I want you to take out your own stories. Look at your writing from yesterday. Today you're going to work with that same wondering part and add some thoughts and feelings that your character is having. Remember, always think about making a good picture in the reader's mind.

Circulate about the room, supporting children as needed, as they continue writing the first part of their stories.

Week 5/Lesson 5

Using Stretching Strategies: Adding Dialogue

Readers Make Good Writers

Story element: character

Dialogue within a piece of writing is directly related to the story element of **character**. Writers use dialogue as an explicit and immediate way of letting the reader know how a character is feeling. A character's statements are a
(continued on page 54)

Lesson Overview

In this final lesson of Week 5, children round out their work on the wondering part by using the third stretching strategy. After teacher modeling and class discussion, children work on adding dialogue to their own stories. At the end of this lesson, children should have good first drafts of one story part, the wondering part. This section should incorporate at least one or two sentences that reflect each of the three stretching strategies. Children will have ample opportunity in weeks 8 and 9 to revise and edit their work, so it is fine if their drafts are still rough and truly works in progress at the end of this week.

Sample Lesson Dialogue and Instruction

Teacher: So far we have worked on two good ways to stretch out the wondering part and really create a picture in the reader's mind. What else can I do when I'm writing a story to help stretch things out and add lots of interest for the reader?

Abby: Have the characters talk to each other.

Teacher: That's right. We call this *dialogue* and we call this stretching strategy "adding dialogue." Dialogue is just a character's words spoken out loud. Usually two or (continued from page 53) window into his or her nature and a unique means of demonstrating relationships among characters.

In *The Other Side*, the dialogue between Clover and Mama shows us how Clover's mother is trying to teach her to behave in a certain way. Dialogue also lets us into the relationship between Clover and Annie. They talk to each other and become friends, questioning their parents' and society's rules.

In *Thank You, Mr. Falker*, the dialogue between Trisha and her peers emphasizes the way Trisha feels about herself. When we hear what the other children say to her, we learn how mean they are. We also learn a lot about Mr. Falker when he finally helps Trisha. When he says, "You poor baby . . . how awful for you to be so lonely and afraid," we get an immediate glimpse into his kind and gentle nature.

more characters are talking, just as if they were having a conversation in real life. Let's look again at the wondering part of my story. [*Display transparency from Week 5/Lesson 2 or write this part on the board (see page 48).*] Do you see dialogue in this part of my story?

Rachel: I see a place where you told us one thing you said.

Teacher: I did do that. Right here. [*Underline the sentence that begins, "Do you think . . ."*] And is there another place?

Leah: Where Scott answers.

Teacher: You've found it. [*Underline the sentence that begins "Then he answered . . ." and point to these two dialogue sentences as you speak.*] What are the big clues here that tell you this is dialogue?

Clara: The words tell you—*I asked* and *he answered*.

Teacher: That's one big clue. Dialogue usually has words that make it clear that someone is talking. One word that is easy to use is *said*. It's okay to use this a few times, but just as I did in my story, writers try to use different words to show someone is saying something. You should try to do that, too. What's the other big clue?

Louis: The punctuation marks?

Teacher: Wow! That's it. Anytime a character speaks directly, there are quotation marks to show readers that these words are being spoken. Does dialogue make you feel like you're there in the story?

Joshua: Yes, it's like we're listening to you and Scott talk.

Teacher: I think so, too, when I read dialogue in a story. Today you're going to put dialogue into your stories. And remember, you're still working on the wondering part. You're keeping your readers wondering and you're building a picture in their minds. That's a lot to think about, but I'm getting the feeling from the work I saw yesterday that you guys really know a lot about writing stories. And I'll be here to help if you need it.

Reassure children that they probably won't remember exactly the words spoken by the people in their stories, but that's fine—they should just take a good guess at recalling what was probably said. Circulate about the room, supporting children as needed, as they continue writing the first part of their stories.

Weeks 6 and 7

Writing Workshop

Along with Week 5, these are the core writing workshop weeks. During this time, children have the chance to actually compose their stories. Children's work during these two weeks follows the pattern established in Week 5. Each Monday you help them examine in-depth a key story part. After some class discussion, children hear two brief stories, one a good example and the other a poor example, of the targeted story part. They meet in small groups to evaluate and select the better story and then, as a whole class and with teacher guidance, they discuss their understanding of what that story part is really all about. In subsequent days, children apply each of the three stretching strategies to the targeted story part. Your sample story continues to provide a model for their own work.

Week 6 focuses on the climax of the story, the critical "hot spot" in which the wondering is resolved and the tension relieved. Week 7 focuses on the closing, in which a well-structured narrative helps readers synthesize their understanding of all that has happened. Each of the two weeks ends with a review day—a chance for children to go back to work on the targeted story part and/or on previous story parts to flesh them out and make them as complete as possible.

One way to help children take on responsibility for completing their writing is to set goals on a class calendar, visible to everyone in the class, for when the different stages of writing need to be completed. This helps children feel accountable for their work as they realize they must finish within the established time frames.

As you continue real story writing during these weeks, it remains critical for children to keep referring to the narratives they have read and heard. Continue to be ready to discuss and review with children all the things they have noticed good writers do in the read alouds you shared during Weeks 1, 2, and 3. The knowledge they have acquired about these story elements should be guiding their decisions as they structure and compose their own stories.

Planning Calendar

Unit Week 6: Week of _____

Monday	Tuesday	Wednesday	Thursday	Friday
Lesson 1: **Focusing on the Story's "Hot Spot"**	*Lesson 2:* **Using Stretching Strategies: Describing the Scene**	*Lesson 3:* **Using Stretching Strategies: Explaining What the Narrator/Main Character Is Thinking and Feeling**	*Lesson 4:* **Using Stretching Strategies: Adding Dialogue**	*Lesson 5:* **Reviewing the Three Stretching Strategies Within the Context of Writing the Hot Spot**
• Review the concept of resolving tension: the hot spot is the most important part of the story	• Review that writers use different strategies to help readers get a good picture of a story in their mind	• Review how explaining what the narrator or main character is thinking and feeling helps readers feel as if they are right there with the characters	• Review how making characters speak in conversation helps readers feel as if they are right there in the story	• Hold a class discussion to review all three stretching strategies
• Present a good example and a poor example of hot spots in sample stories	• Discuss how to use the "describing the scene" strategy within a story's hot spot	• Model how to "explain what the narrator/main character is thinking and feeling"	• Model how to "add dialogue"	• Check in with students about progress on their story's hot spot
• Students evaluate these stories and explain their choices	• Model using the "describing the scene" strategy	• Students use this strategy to stretch their hot spot	• Students use this stretching strategy in their hot spot	• Give students, as needed, the opportunity to go back to their writing and continue to stretch out the hot spot (and the wondering part if that still needs work) using the three strategies
	• Students use this strategy in their hot spot			
Story elements tie-in: plot, movement through time, change	**Story element tie-in: setting**	**Story element tie-in: character**	**Story element tie-in: character**	

Planning Calendar

Unit Week 7: Week of _____

Monday	Tuesday	Wednesday	Thursday	Friday
Lesson 1: **Focusing on the Story's Closing**	*Lesson 2:* **Using Stretching Strategies: Describing the Scene**	*Lesson 3:* **Using Stretching Strategies: Explaining What the Narrator/Main Character Is Thinking and Feeling**	*Lesson 4:* **Using Stretching Strategies: Adding Dialogue**	*Lesson 5:* **Reviewing the Three Stretching Strategies Within the Context of Writing the Closing**
• Review the concept of a story's need for a closing	• Review the types of endings discussed	• Review how explaining what the narrator or main character is thinking and feeling helps readers feel as if they are right there with the characters	• Review how making characters speak in conversation helps readers feel as if they are right there in the story	• Hold a class discussion to review all three stretching strategies
• Discuss the types of closings applicable to a story, especially to a personal narrative	• Review that writers use different strategies to help readers get a good picture of a story in their mind	• Model how to "explain what the narrator/main character is thinking and feeling" within the story's closing	• Model how to "add dialogue" within the story's closing	• Check in with students about progress on their story's closing
• Present a good example and a poor example of closings	• Discuss how to use the "describing the scene" strategy within a story's closing	• Students use this strategy to stretch the closing in their stories	• Students use this strategy to stretch the closing in their stories	• Give students, as needed, the opportunity to go back to their writing and continue to stretch out the closing (and the wondering part and hot spot if those still need work) using the three strategies
• Students evaluate these stories and explain their choices	• Model using the "describing the scene" strategy			
Story elements tie-in: character, plot, movement through time, change	• Students use this strategy to stretch their closing			

Using Picture Books to Teach Narrative Writing SCHOLASTIC TEACHING RESOURCES

Focusing on the Story's "Hot Spot"

Lesson Overview

Much like in Week 5/Lesson 1, this lesson focuses on developing children's understanding of a key part of the story plan. Here the focus is on the **hot spot**, or climax, of the story. After some initial discussion and analysis of the hot spot, children read two simple stories, one that incorporates a good example of a hot spot and the other that has no hot spot at all. In small groups, children evaluate the stories then join a class discussion to review their choices and, with your guidance, reinforce their understanding of this critical story component.

This lesson launches a week of work focused on children's own writing. They will have the opportunity in the ensuing days to put into action their new knowledge of what makes a good hot spot.

Sample Lesson Dialogue and Instruction

Teacher: You worked so hard last week on getting the wondering part in your stories stretched out and full. Your stories are really coming along! Today we're ready to move on to the next part of the story. Who can tell me what it's called? [*Point to the display chart of the labeled story plan.*]

Carla: The hot spot.

Teacher: That's it. We're up to the hot spot. This is such an important part of the story. You could even say it's the most important part of all because readers finally find out what they've been waiting for since the promise sentence. In my story, it's the moment that Scott and I arrived at the island of Capri. Do you think after they read the hot spot, readers are still wondering?

John: No! You told them what happened.

Teacher: Good! You guys are really catching on to story structure. So just the way I did last week, today I'm going to share with you two examples of stories. One example is not very good. It doesn't have a hot spot at all. The other example is of a better story. Your job is to figure out which one is good and be able to explain why.

Readers Make Good Writers

Story elements: *plot, movement through time, change*

At this crucial stage in the writing process, the story elements of **plot, movement through time,** and **change** come into play. The plot, which has been developing throughout the story, reaches its peak moment and usually reveals the key change or transformation that the story is really about. It is in the hot spot that the writer resolves the tension that has been building all along. Time plays a new role at this moment, too, as events that have been steadily unfolding reach a crescendo. Readers discover whether the character achieves what he or she has been striving for.

In *The Other Side*, the hot spot occurs

(continued on page 59)

(continued from page 58)
when the girls approach the fence, introduce themselves, and smile at each other. It is everything that readers have been waiting and hoping for. Things will never be the same for these two girls.

In *Thank You, Mr. Falker*, the hot spot is more dramatic. When Trisha sobs because she has been teased mercilessly about not being able to read and Mr. Falker consoles her—"We're going to change all that, girl. You're going to read— I promise you that"— readers feel like cheering. All the events we have witnessed in the story so far, from first through fifth grade, culminate here. From this point on, Trisha begins the change that results in her learning how to read.

Organize the class into partners or small groups. Read aloud, or write on a transparency or chalkboard, the following story examples:

One day, Scott asked me to meet him at a fancy restaurant for dinner. The restaurant was in New York. I thought that would be fun, so I said yes. I had never been to that restaurant before. I was really looking forward to it. Then I went. When we left the restaurant, I took a taxi back to my apartment because it was raining very hard. I thought to myself that I had enjoyed my evening with Scott very much.

My sister came to visit me at my new house. I was really excited about seeing her. I hoped we would do lots of fun things together. When she finally arrived, it was the best day I can remember. I met her at the airport and gave her a big hug. We went shopping, we went out to eat, and we rented funny movies that made us laugh and laugh. It was a great vacation for my sister.

After children have evaluated these stories, bring the class together to share their opinions. Guide the discussion so that children correctly identify the second story as the good example and that they are clear about what constitutes a hot spot and why it is essential to a story's success.

Teacher: Now we all know why a hot spot is so important to a good story. A story without a hot spot feels like it has a hole right in the middle, doesn't it? That's because something big is missing. During this week we're going to spend lots of time really stretching out the hot spot in our stories. You'll use every one of the three stretching strategies that you learned last week. Because your hot spot needs to be the most interesting part of your story, you need to be really thoughtful and make an especially good picture for the reader.

Special Note

For the next three days—Tuesday, Wednesday, and Thursday—of Week 6, the lessons follow the same instructional pattern for applying the stretching strategies as was established in Week 5. You might start each of these lessons by saying, "Today we're going to continue to stretch out the hot-spot part of our stories. We want to make readers feel like they are there with us in our story. Let's go back to what we wrote in our previous lesson." Take off from that point, using your own sample story to model for children how to apply each stretching strategy to the hot spot in their own stories.

The planning calendar on page 56 provides the lesson focus and specific instructional goals for each of these three lessons. You can use the sample dialogue scripts in Week 5 for the equivalent lessons as models for instruction of the stretching strategies within the hot spot.

As in Week 5, the sample story's hot spot, below, uses **boldface** to indicate the "describing the scene" stretching strategy; *italics* to show the strategy for thoughts and feelings of the character; and <u>underlining</u> for the "adding dialogue" stretching strategy. Refer to the story plan to point out the hot spot, as shown below:

- ## We arrived at the island. (hot spot)

Hot Spot in Sample Story

After what felt like hours, the captain finally announced that we were arriving. I got so excited I jumped out of my seat and ran to the front of the boat.

In the distance I saw it—Capri! It was large and green with hills rolling along the sides. The water surrounding the island was sparkling blue. The beaches looked beautiful. *I knew I would love Capri.*

<u>I looked at Scott as we pulled into the dock and smiled. "We're here," I whispered. He smiled back and exclaimed, "I don't think you're going to be disappointed. It looks extraordinary!"</u>

The final day of Week 6, Friday, is an opportunity for children to revisit, as necessary, their work on using all three strategies to stretch the hot spot in their stories. See page 56 for the lesson focus and instructional goals for this lesson. If children are satisfied with their story's hot spot, they may want to revisit the wondering part to make sure it is as full as they want it to be.

Focusing on the Story's Closing

Readers Make Good Writers

Story elements: *character, plot, movement through time, change*

Because a story's closing describes how everything wraps up, it calls into play the **plot's** events and typically the **change** at the core of the story. The story element **movement through time** is also important because the closing demonstrates how the **characters** have developed up to this particular point. The closing usually includes a character's feeling, a reference back to the beginning of the story, or sometimes an expectation for the future.

In *The Other Side*, the closing is simple but eloquent: "... we sat up on the fence, all of us in a long line." The phrase "all of us"

(continued on page 62)

Lesson Overview

Similar to the first lessons in Weeks 5 and 6, this lesson deepens children's understanding of a key story part—in this case, a story's closing. After initial discussion of two kinds of typical closings for personal narratives, children consider two simple stories, one that incorporates a good example of a closing based on a character's feelings, and another that has no closing at all. In small groups, children evaluate the stories then join a class discussion to review their choices and, with your guidance, reinforce their understanding of this important story component.

Next, you visit the alternate kind of closing—the circle closing. Children listen to a story that exemplifies this kind of pattern and discuss it as a class.

This lesson launches a week of work focused on children's own writing. They will have the opportunity in the ensuing days to put into action their new knowledge of what makes a good closing.

Sample Lesson Dialogue and Instruction

Teacher: This week is another exciting one—you're going to work on finishing up your stories. We've all got our promise sentence, our wondering part, and our hot spot. Now we're ready to take on the last story part on our story plan. The name of this part means "ending." Here it is on the chart. *[Point to the display chart of the labeled story plan.]* Who wants to read this word?

Ben: It says *closing*.

Teacher: That's exactly right. We're now ready to write the closing for our stories. But first I've got to ask you something. I thought we already told our readers what they've been wondering about. We already gave them the answer, didn't we? *[Use transparency of the sample story and point to the word* finally *in the sentence, "After what felt like hours, the captain finally announced that we were arriving" at the beginning of the hot spot.]* What word is this?

Josh: *Finally!*

(continued from page 61) speaks volumes. And the final exchange between Annie and Clover is imbued with their new, shared feeling of hope: "Someday somebody's going to come along and knock this old fence down."

The closing in *Thank You, Mr. Falker*, is especially significant and beautiful. Trisha is finally able to hold a book in her hand joyfully because she knows she'll be able to read it. This ending has characteristics of both a circle closing and a closing based on a character's feelings. The grandpa's poetic quotation about knowledge, books, and honey is repeated from the first page, thus bringing readers full circle. At the same time, the very last sentence is all about feeling: ". . . they weren't tears of sadness—she was happy, so very happy."

Teacher: Yes, that's a word that I used in my hot spot and that I know a lot of you have used, too. And look at this. I see the word *finally* again. *[Display transparency of the "good hot spot" sample story on page 60 and point to the word finally.]* It's a great word for a hot spot. It tells readers that this is what they've been waiting for. But here's the tricky part. *Finally* means "the end." So, is the hot spot the end of your story?

Elizabeth: No, because the closing comes after the hot spot.

Teacher: I guess I'm not tricking you! *Finally* means the end of the wondering. But it's not actually the end of the story. Something else has to happen to close the story. Imagine you had a slice of pizza for lunch, but it had no crust. Would you feel satisfied that you got a whole slice of pizza? Of course not! That's what the closing is like—just as you know your pizza is done when you've eaten the crust, the closing lets the reader know the story is finished.

Sam: That makes sense. I wouldn't enjoy my pizza if it had no crust.

Teacher: That's a good way to put it! There are a few ways that writers can create a closing for a personal narrative. One way they can end their piece is with a feeling. A second way is to go back to the beginning of the piece and use the first sentence as the ending, too. That's called a circle ending.

Larry: Because it makes you look back at the beginning?

Teacher: Yes, and connect it, just like you do in a circle. We're going to look at examples of both kinds today. Let's start the kind of closing that includes a feeling. I'm going to show you two examples of stories. One example has no closing. The other example has a great closing. Your job is to figure out which one is good and be able to explain why. Remember, the closing here is the feeling kind, not the circle kind.

Divide the class into partners or small groups. Read aloud, or write on a transparency or chalkboard, the following story examples:

On Halloween my friends and I decided to get dressed up together. We all wore big blue wigs and long black dresses. We went to a party that was giving a prize for the best costume. We hoped all night that we would win. We danced and talked to friends. The whole evening we couldn't wait to hear if we would win the prize. At 9:00 the winner was finally announced! "And the winners are . . . Naomi and her friends." We couldn't believe it. We won the prize—a free movie for all of us. We jumped up and down and hugged one another. When the party was over we walked home with big smiles on our faces. It was the best Halloween we ever had.

On Halloween my friends and I decided to get dressed up together. We all wore big blue wigs and long black dresses. We went to a party that was giving a prize for the best costume. We hoped all night that we would win, but we didn't really think we had a chance. We danced and talked to friends. We took lots of pictures. The whole evening we couldn't wait to hear if would win the prize. At 9:00 the winner was finally announced! We held our breath while they made the announcement. "And the winners are . . . Naomi and her friends." We couldn't believe it. We won. Then we went home.

After children have evaluated these stories, bring the class together to share their opinions. Guide the discussion so that children correctly identify the first story as a good example and that they are clear about what constitutes a closing and why it is essential to a story's success.

Teacher: Now we all know how to recognize one kind of closing. I'm going to show you one more story. This one has a great closing but it's a different kind. It's the circle kind. Listen carefully.

Display a transparency or write on the chalkboard the following story and read it aloud to the class. After presenting the story, call on a volunteer to point to the ending and the beginning sentences. Discuss the difference between the two kinds of closings.

Jennifer and Karen became instant friends. Jennifer had been nervous and excited about the first day of school. She didn't know anyone because she had just moved to town and she wondered if she would make any friends. When she walked into the classroom, she looked from one face to another and nothing was familiar. None of the children seemed interested in her. Jennifer suddenly saw another little girl standing alone. She had long dark curls just

like hers. She looked a little scared, too. Jennifer decided to be brave. She straightened her skirt, gave a big smile and walked right up to the girl. "Hi," Jennifer said. "I'm new here. My name is Jennifer." Jennifer waited for the girl to say something. "I am so glad you came over to me. I'm new here, too, and I was hoping to make a friend. My name is Karen." That was it. Jennifer and Karen spent the whole day getting to know each other. They had lunch together and talked a lot. Jennifer and Karen became instant friends.

Teacher: Now you're really ready to tackle writing a closing for your stories. During this week you'll be stretching out the closing, using the strategies we've learned.

Special Note

For the next three days—Tuesday, Wednesday, and Thursday—of Week 7, the lessons follow the same instructional pattern for applying the stretching strategies as was established in Week 5. You might start each of these lessons by saying, "Today we're going to continue to stretch out the closing parts of our stories. We want to make readers feel like they are there with us in our story. Let's go back to what we wrote in our previous lesson." Take off from that point, using your own sample story to model for children how to apply each stretching strategy to their closing.

The planning calendar on page 57 provides the lesson focus and specific instructional goals for each of these three lessons. You can use the sample dialogue scripts in Week 5 for the equivalent lessons as models for instruction of the stretching strategies within the closing.

Additionally, you might point out that because your sample story included a good deal of feeling and thinking, you have decided to create a closing focused on feeling, not a circle closing. Help children realize that you made your choice based on the nature of your own story; they will each need to find the right ending for their own stories. Help them understand, too, that the closing does not have to be as elaborate as the hot spot or the wondering part. Just a few sentences may be sufficient.

With the same conventions used in Weeks 5 and 6 (**boldface** to indicate the "describing the scene" stretching strategy; *italics* to show the strategy for conveying the thoughts and feelings of the character; and underlining for the "adding dialogue" stretching strategy), the sample story's closing appears below as well as the closing part of the story plan.

- Scott and I went to the beach on Capri. **(closing)**

Closing in Sample Story

We walked out of the boat and down the ramp. We walked through the winding streets and went straight to the beach. The soft, warm sand slipped through our feet. "It's everything I pictured and even better!" I burst out to Scott. *I was smiling from ear to ear. I knew we were going to have a great day on the island of Capri.*

The final day of Week 7, Friday, is an opportunity for children to revisit, as necessary, their work on using all three strategies to stretch the closing in their stories. See page 57 for the lesson focus and instructional goals for this lesson. If children are satisfied with their story's closing, they may want to revisit the wondering part or the hot spot to make sure they are as full as they need to be.

Weeks 8 and 9

Revising, Editing, and Publishing

I t's a good idea to allot at least a week for children to revise and then edit their drafts. Week 8 is set up to include two revision lessons and three editing lessons, but you can vary this according to your own class's needs. This is the next step toward children having completed products that they will be able to share proudly with peers and family. As such, it's another important week of learning the writing process.

The lessons you teach for this unit of study can provide children the basis for how to revise most of the writing they will do throughout the year. Of course there will be certain features that are specific to each genre, but general revision strategies work well for most of the writing children will do.

While revising allows children to fill in gaps and check that their stories read well and make sense, editing gives them the chance to make their stories "look right." This is the time to correct spelling and punctuation errors and to attend to the other mechanics. Editing can happen only after revising because when writers revise, they work on the actual words in the piece, and when they edit they are in essence cleaning up the way that writing looks.

By Week 9, the last week in the workshop, children are finally ready to publish. Because it is challenging for many children to copy over their work neatly, it's a good idea to allow a full week for the publishing stage. Children spend a busy final week indeed—copying their work, illustrating it, and, with your help, formatting it into a booklet. But the hard work pays off, and at the end of this week, there's no doubt that you—and they—will be truly proud. And to cap off the whole workshop, the final lesson offers children a chance to revisit the narrative story elements they have incorporated into their stories and to evaluate their own and others' work using a special checklist.

Planning Calendar

Unit Week 8: Week of ____

Monday	Tuesday	Wednesday	Thursday	Friday
Lesson 1: **Introducing Revision**	*Lesson 2:* **Continuing Revision**	*Lesson 3:* **Introducing Editing**	*Lesson 4:* **Continuing Editing**	*Lesson 5:* **Continuing Revising and Editing**
• Discuss how writers know when a story is finished	• Continue discussing revision	• Discuss further the difference between editing and revising	• Continue discussing the editing process	• Students continue revising and editing their stories
• Encourage students to think about these questions: Does my story sound right? Does it make sense?	• Students continue revising their stories per guidelines and checklist	• Explain that editing focuses on the mechanics or "look" of the text	• Students continue editing their stories per guidelines and checklists	• Provide students with individual copies of the three checklists (revising, editing, and spelling) for their ongoing reference
• Help students understand the difference between revising and editing	• Circulate as necessary to guide students' work	• Review your model story and look for places for editing	• Circulate as necessary to guide students' work	
• Create and display Revising Checklist		• Model how you make corrections to the text		
• Review your model story and look for places for revision		• Create and display Editing Checklist		
• Model reading the story out loud and making corrections to the text		• Introduce the Spelling Checklist		
		• Students start editing their stories		

Planning Calendar

Unit Week 9: Week of _____

Monday	Tuesday	Wednesday	Thursday	Friday
Lesson 1: **Introducing the Idea of Publishing**	*Lesson 2:* **Continuing Publishing**	*Lesson 3:* **Continuing Publishing**	*Lesson 4:* **Continuing Publishing**	*Lesson 5:* **Publishing**
• Introduce the concept of publishing • Discuss how writers ask these questions before publishing a piece: *Does my story make sense? Does it sound right? Does it look right?* • Examine published texts with students • Create a chart with criteria for publishing • Distribute a prepared published copy of your model story • Students start working on publishing	• Refer to the chart and review the characteristics of a published piece • Students continue working on publishing	• Students continue working on publishing • Review importance of illustrations • Encourage students to make illustrations for their stories	• Students continue working on publishing • Students continue illustrating their stories • Help students create a cover and staple together their stories	• Discuss and reflect on the entire unit • Invite students to share their work with one another • Distribute a copy of the Publishing Checklist for Story Elements Checklist to each student • Encourage students to review one another's work using the checklist • Celebrate the work your students have successfully completed!

Introducing Revision

Lesson Overview

This introductory lesson to revising gives children a chance to step back from their stories and evaluate them for completion. Together as a class, discuss what makes a writing piece complete. Also, identify the process of editing and differentiate it from revising so that children realize they'll have yet another opportunity to focus on mechanics such as spelling. As part of the discussion, enlist children's help in generating a checklist of key points to look for during revision. This checklist becomes a display chart that children can refer to on an ongoing basis as they revise their work. Photocopy the checklist for children's individual use. To reinforce the concept of revising, use your model story to demonstrate how you check for completion and make your own revisions. Children can then launch right into their own revising.

Sample Lesson Dialogue and Instruction

Teacher: You have all been working so hard on your stories. You have planned, stretched each story part, and really spent time making great stories. Today we need to start thinking about finishing up the stories. How do you know when your piece is done?

Emma: You've told the readers everything they need to know.

Teacher: Absolutely. That's one important thing. What else?

Jack: It has a closing.

Teacher: Yes, what else?

Taylor: Make sure all of the words are spelled right.

Teacher: Yes—you know, you've just listed some of the really important ways writers get their pieces ready to share with the world. There are two big processes we need to do this week to make sure our stories are ready to be published. The first is called *revision* or *revising*, and the second is called *editing*. This lesson is going to be about revision. We'll think about editing later this week. *[Label a blank chart "Revising Checklist." As you and the class discuss and define each feature of revision, add it to the chart. See page 77 for a sample completed chart.]* Some of the things you just said belong on this chart.

	Emma's idea about making sure you have told the reader everything they need to know is one of them. And so is the one about checking to see if we have a closing. When we revise, we are thinking about the ideas in the story. We are not worried about spelling yet. So I'm going to save Taylor's really good suggestion for our editing lessons. What else belongs on our revising chart?
Ian:	Did you put all of the words in your story?
Teacher:	Yes! That is a great one. Many times I'll read one of your stories and I'll see that you have forgotten a word here or there. So it doesn't sound right when we read it. Anything else?
Paul:	Do we need to look at the stretching strategies we used in our story?
Teacher:	Absolutely. You worked really hard on making a picture for the reader. You need to check your writing to see that you included the stretching strategies we have talked about.
Laura:	Do we need to look for all the story parts?
Teacher:	Yes, you do, because they're all important. We already mentioned the closing, but you also need to check for the promise sentence, the wondering part, and the hot spot. There are a lot of important questions you can ask yourself about revising. But there's one big question to ask yourself that will help you know if you are done: "Does my story make sense?" If you can answer yes, then it is probably revised well.

Complete the revision chart by including two additional statements that allow for children to record their work with a partner (see page 77). Model using these revision strategies in your own sample story. (You might want to modify the story ahead of time so that there is something that actually needs revising.) Demonstrate how you read the story out loud and use the chart to look for errors. Conclude the lesson by distributing copies of the Revising Checklist and having children begin revising their own writing. Reassure them that they will have additional time to finish revisions tomorrow. Then they will work with a partner who will confirm that their revisions are finished.

Note: The next day's lesson, Week 8/Lesson 2, offers children a second opportunity to revise their story.

Introducing Editing

Lesson Overview

Now that children's stories have been revised and made as complete as possible, they are ready to tackle the final writing task—editing. After this, their stories will be ready for publishing. Follow a similar instructional pattern for this lesson as you used in the introductory revising lesson. Together as a class, discuss what makes a writing piece "look right." Invite children to help you generate a checklist of key points to look for during editing. This checklist becomes a display chart that children can refer to on an ongoing basis as they edit their work. Photocopy the Editing Checklist for children's individual use. Distribute and discuss a special Spelling Checklist for children to use during their editing as well. To reinforce the concept of editing, use your model story to demonstrate how you check for errors and make your own corrections. Be sure to model use of the Spelling Checklist as part of your editing. Children can then launch right into their own editing, which they will continue through two more lessons.

Sample Lesson Dialogue and Instruction

Teacher: For the past few days you have been revising your pieces and getting them ready to share with the world. I told you there were two things you needed to do to your work before you publish it. Revision was one and editing is the next. If you think about what you just did to your work to get it ready, what do you think the next step will be?

Avery: I think we need to make sure it's neat so other people can read it.

Teacher: Interesting. What else do you think we need to do so our work is ready for other people to read it?

Charles: Make sure it's all spelled right.

Teacher: Good, you are thinking like editors. Editing means making sure the piece looks right. So when I say "looks right," what does that include? Let's make a chart for editing. *[Label a blank chart "Editing." As you and the class discuss and define each feature of editing, add it to the chart. See page 77 for a sample completed chart.]* One thing you mentioned is spelling. Of course we

	need to make sure all of our words are spelled right for people to be able to read our work. That's something we can list on our editing chart, but it's so important that I have a special Spelling Checklist I'm going to give you. Let's talk more about spelling in just a bit. What else can we add to our editing list?
Monica:	How about periods and that kind of stuff?
Teacher:	Yes, you mean punctuation—all of the marks that come at the end of a sentence. Punctuation also includes quotation marks. I know you will have those in your piece because we all tried using dialogue. One more thing you need to really pay attention to is making sure that you have lowercase and capital letters in all of the right spots. So, let's add all this to our editing chart. [*Write these editing points and additional big question; see page 77.*] I just did something to this chart I hadn't told you about. What was it?
Conor:	You added "Big Question" at the bottom.
Teacher:	You're very observant! Yes, just the way I did on the Revising Checklist, I added a special big question at the end of this chart. After checking all the little questions, if you can answer that your piece looks right, then you have probably edited it well. [*Complete the Editing Checklist by including two additional statements that allow for children to record their work with a partner. Distribute photocopied versions of this chart to children and explain that they will use this checklist as they edit individually and with partners over the next few days.*]
Teacher:	Now, before I show you how I edit my own piece and get you started editing your own, I want to talk more about spelling.

Distribute photocopies to each child of the Spelling Checklist (page 78). Walk children through the process you expect them to follow for correcting spelling words during editing. Remind them first to refer to the word wall. Children should be able to locate many of the words they have used in their stories right on the word wall. If they cannot find a word, have them use the Spelling Checklist to try out several possible spellings. After writing their initial spelling, children get two more tries to get a word right. Sometimes they will recognize a correct spelling after one try; at other times they will still need help after two tries. They may also decide, after trying on their own, to check with a friend who knows the word or to look it up in a dictionary. In an individual conference before publishing, you should check all spellings and correct any remaining errors so that the published work will be exact.

Note that it's important to plan a conference with each child during the editing phase. You want to make sure each story is truly ready before children copy it over and publish it the following week. It isn't realistic to expect the stories to be perfect—despite children's best efforts at revising and editing—when they show it to you. There will be things they overlook. That's where you come in. Make any necessary corrections on this current rough draft.

Week 9/Lesson 1

Introducing the Idea of Publishing

Lesson Overview

This lesson introduces children to the publishing process. For young children, publishing means taking a revised and edited story and copying it over as neatly as possible so that it is transformed into a final draft with no errors. Publishing is also the time for children to illustrate their work and to add a cover. In this first lesson, children examine published books and suggest criteria that must be met in order for a story to be a "published work." This criteria list becomes another chart that they can refer to during their work. Have available photocopies of your own sample story, neatly transcribed, illustrated, stapled, and published that you can share with the class as a model. Children are then ready to begin this final, exciting phase—publishing their own stories!

Sample Lesson Dialogue and Instruction

Teacher: You have been working so hard on revising and editing your pieces. It feels like we are just about ready to publish our work. Publishing is the last step in writing. It means getting your stories all ready to share with the world. When you are sure you can answer all of these questions, then you are ready to publish. [*Write on the board or display a transparency of the following three questions.*]

- Does my story make sense?
- Does my story sound right?
- Does my story look right?

Teacher:	Do you see any surprises in that list?
James:	No! Those are the questions you told us about last week.
Teacher:	That's right. These are the exact things you've been working on during revising and editing. So when you are sure your answer to all those questions is "yes" and you are ready to publish, what do you need to do next? Well, there are some special things to think about. Let's look at a story from our basket of stories and see what we notice about the published work. [*Select a narrative picture book from the story basket and examine it with the class.*] What do you see that this writer did to make it a published piece?
Emma:	There are no mistakes.
Jack:	It has pictures.
Charles:	It is neat.
Teacher:	Wow, you guys know a lot about writing! You need to

My grandPar-ents came to N.H. We played tag. I wondered if I was going to tag them. My grandMother said ready set go. I was running. My grandParents ran away through the trees. I was running through the grasus. The sun was shining. I was trying to get My grandParents fo'r a very long time. I was running though bushes. I was running through trees. It was hot. I ran over bridges. We ran-

around and around and around and around a lot of times. We ran near trees a lot of times. I couldn't wait to tag My grandParents. It was summer. I was very hot. I was sweating very much. I was out of breath. Finally after a very long time I tagged them. I shouted "I won!" I was so so so happy. I did a boogie dance. I put My arms out I had beaten My grandParents. Finally after a few days I went home.

think about all of those things when you publish. You'll be copying over your piece without any mistakes. Illustrations, or pictures, can go with your work if you like. Let's make a list of publishing ideas so you know exactly what you need to do to your story. I'm going to list what you've already told me and add a few more important things. [*Write and display the following chart.*]

Published Work

- No mistakes
- Neat
- Illustrations match the words
- Best handwriting
- Has a cover with title and author's name on it
- Copied on special publishing paper
- Pages stapled together

After reading through the chart together, distribute to each child a prepared photocopy of your own model story. Make sure it meets all the criteria on the chart. Allow time for children to look through it and invite volunteers to read it aloud. Children will be excited to see this final version and be even more motivated to get started on their own publishing efforts.

During the remainder of the lesson, invite children to start their own publishing. Provide special, good-quality paper and encourage them to use their neatest handwriting. It is a challenge for many

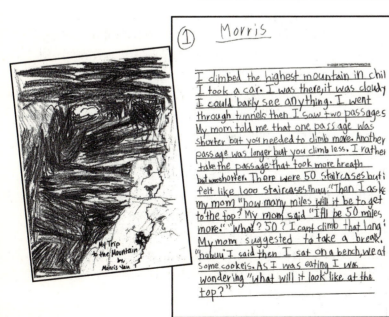

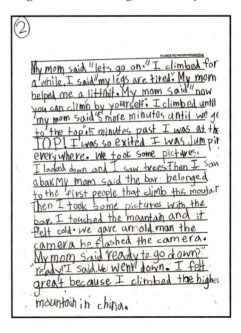

young children to copy over their work neatly, so let them know they have the rest of the week to accomplish this task.

Note: The next days' lessons, Lessons 2, 3, and 4, offer children further opportunities to get their story ready for publishing. During these days they complete the copying and then add illustrations to their work. They can draw the illustrations directly on the story pages or on separate pages that can be attached. The final lesson is a special sharing day as described in the Special Note below.

Special Note

The final lesson of the workshop is an opportunity for peer evaluation and peer celebration. Rather than presenting a formal lesson, tell children that today will be a special day for sharing, reading, and celebrating. Distribute several photocopies of the Publishing Checklist for Story Elements (page 79) to each child. This checklist is especially valuable to use at the end of this unit because it employs the narrative story-element terms. It circles back to the beginning of this workshop when children were first reading personal narrative books and just learning the five key elements of character, plot, setting, movement through time, and change. Their own stories are now ready to be evaluated according to those same terms. This is quite an accomplishment.

Pair children and have each partner read the other's story (or read their own story aloud to their partner). Then have partners fill out the checklist. Be very clear that this is a time for praise and that today's sharing and comments should include only compliments for others' stories. Remind children that there's always something good to be said and that doing so is one way to help each other celebrate. Once they have shared with one partner, children should rotate to do the same thing with other classmates. It's definitely helpful for each child to hear from more than one peer.

This might also be a day to invite children's families or other classes to visit for similar sharing. Invite family members and children from other classes to fill out the same comments sheet. You can't do this for every publication, but it's a wonderful way to celebrate a few times a year. The important thing to remember, whatever way you choose to celebrate, is that your students are now able writers who can use story elements to structure their stories and who can talk about narratives comfortably and knowledgeably. They have come such a long way since the first week. They are published writers!

Revising Checklist

____ My story tells readers everything I want them to know.
____ My story has all the words it needs and it sounds right.
____ I used the three stretching strategies in my story.
____ My story includes all the story parts.

Big Question:

____ Does my story make sense?

Partner Work:

____ I read my story out loud to my partner.
____ My partner agrees with this checklist.

Editing Checklist

____ All words are spelled right.
____ All punctuation is correct.
____ Quotation marks are used in the right places.
____ Capital letters and lowercase letters are in the right places.

Big Question:

____ Does my story look right?

Partner Work:

____ I read my story out loud to my partner.
____ My partner agrees with this checklist.

Spelling Checklist

My Spelling	First Try	Second Try	Book Spelling
frend	freind	freand	friend

Using Picture Books to Teach Narrative Writing Scholastic Teaching Resources

Publishing Checklist for Story Elements

_____ This story has **characters**.
Name one: _____

_____ This story has a **setting**.
Where is it? Fill out the umbrella.

_____ This story has a **plot**.
The plot is
Beginning: _____
Middle: _____
End: _____

_____ This story shows **movement through time**.
How much time passes in the story? _____

_____ This story includes a **change**.
Describe the change: _____
_____

Comments: Write something else about the story that you really liked.
_____
_____
_____

Bibliography

Professional Resources

Anderson, Carl. *How's It Going? A Practical Guide to Conferring with Student Writers*. Portsmouth, NH: Heinemann, 2000.

Anderson, Carl. *Assessing Writers*. Portsmouth, NH: Heinemann, 2005.

Atwell, Nancie. *Lessons That Change Writers*. Portsmouth, NH: FirstHand, 2002.

Calkins, Lucy McCormick. *The Art of Teaching Reading*. New York: Addison Wesley Longman, 2001.

Calkins, Lucy McCormick. *The Art of Teaching Writing*. Portsmouth, NH: FirstHand, 2001.

Calkins, Lucy McCormick. *Units of Study for Primary Writing: A Yearlong Curriculum*. The Teachers College Reading and Writing Project. Portsmouth, NH: FirstHand, 2003.

Davis, Judy, and Sharon Hill. *The No-Nonsense Guide to Teaching Writing: Strategies, Structures, and Solutions*. Portsmouth, NH: Heinemann, 2003.

Fletcher, Ralph. *A Writer's Notebook: Unlocking the Writer Within You*. New York: HarperTrophy, 1996.

Fletcher, Ralph, and Joann Portalupi. *Craft Lessons: Teaching Writing K–8*. Portland, ME: Stenhouse Publishers, 1998.

Fletcher, Ralph, and Joann Portalupi. *Teaching the Qualities of Writing*. Portsmouth, NH: FirstHand, 2004.

Fletcher, Ralph, and Joanne Portalupi. *Writing Workshop: The Essential Guide*. Portsmouth, NH: Heinemann, 2001.

Graves, Donald H. *A Fresh Look at Writing*. Portsmouth, NH: Heinemann, 1994.

Gutkind, Lee. *The Art of Creative Nonfiction: Writing and Selling the Literature of Reality*. New York: John Wiley and Sons, 1997.

Heard, Georgia. *The Revision Toolbox: Teaching Techniques That Work*. Portsmouth, NH: Heinemann, 2002.

Hindley, Joanne. *In the Company of Children*. Portland, ME: Stenhouse Publishers, 1996.

Keene, Ellin Oliver, and Susan Zimmermann. *Mosaic of Thought: Teaching Comprehension in a Reader's Workshop*. Portsmouth, NH: Heinemann, 1997.

Ray, Katie Wood. *What You Know by Heart: How to Develop Curriculum for Your Writing Workshop*. Portsmouth, NH: Heinemann, 2002.

Ray, Katie Wood. *The Writing Workshop: Working Through the Hard Parts (And They're All Hard Parts)*. Urbana, IL: National Council of Teachers of English, 2001.

Recommended Narrative Picture Books

Books with strong examples of characters:

Blume, Judy. *The Pain and the Great One*. New York: Bantam Doubleday Dell, 1973.

Bunting, Eve. *My Big Boy Bed*. New York: Clarion Books, 2003.

Child, Lauren. *I Am Not Sleepy and I Will Not Go to Bed*. Cambridge, MA: Candlewick Press, 2001.

DePaola, Tomie. *Nana Upstairs & Nana Downstairs*. New York: Penguin Group, 1973.

Fox, Mem. *Wilfrid Gordon McDonald Partridge*. La Jolla, CA: Kane/Miller Book Publishers, 1985.

Gray, Libba Moore. *My Mama Had a Dancing Heart*. New York: Orchard Books, 1995.

Hesse, Karen. *Come On, Rain!* New York: Scholastic Inc., 1999.

Parton, Dolly. *Coat of Many Colors*. New York: HarperCollins, 1994.

Polacco, Patricia. *Thank You, Mr. Falker*. New York: Philomel Books, 1998.

Viorst, Judith. *Earrings!* New York: Aladdin Paperbacks, 1990.

Woodson, Jacqueline. *The Other Side*. New York: G.P. Putnam's Sons, 2001.

Books with strong examples of settings:

Aragon, Jane Chelsea. *Salt Hands*. New York: Puffin Unicorn, 1990.

Brinckloe, Julie. *Fireflies*. New York: Aladdin Paperbacks, 1990.

Crews, Donald. *Bigmama's*. New York: Greenwillow Books, 1991.

Crews, Donald. *Shortcut*. New York: Greenwillow Books, 1992.

Good, Elaine W. *Fall Is Here! I Love It!* Intercourse, PA: Good Books, 1994.

Johnson, Angela. *The Leaving Morning*. New York: Orchard Books, 1992.

Keats, Ezra Jack. *The Snowy Day*. New York: Viking Penguin Inc., 1962.

Rylant, Cynthia. *When I Was Young in the Mountains*. New York: Puffin Unicorn, 1992.

Yolen, Jane. *Owl Moon*. New York: Philomel Books, 1987.

Yolen, Jane. *Soft House*. Cambridge, MA: Candlewick Press, 2005.

Books with strong examples of plot:

Crews, Donald. *Shortcut*. New York: Greenwillow Books, 1992.

Danziger, Paula. *Barfburger Baby, I Was Here First*. New York: G.P. Putnam's Sons, 2004.

Greenfield, Eloise. *She Come Bringing Me That Little Baby Girl*. New York: HarperTrophy, 1974.

Howard, Elizabeth Fitzgerald. *Aunt Flossie's Hats (and Crab Cakes Later)*. New York: Clarion Books, 1991.

Polacco, Patricia. *Just Plain Fancy*. New York: Dragonfly Books, 1990.

Polacco, Patricia. *Thunder Cake*. New York: Philomel Books, 1990.

Tavares, Matt. *Zachary's Ball*. Cambridge, MA: Candlewick Press, 2000.

Woodson, Jacqueline. *The Other Side*. New York: G.P. Putnam's Sons, 2001.

Yolen, Jane. *Owl Moon*. New York: Philomel Books, 1987.

Books with strong examples of movement through time:

Bridges, Shirin Yim. *Ruby's Wish*. San Francisco, CA: Chronicle Books, 2002.

Edwards, Becky. *My First Day at Nursery School*. New York: Bloomsbury Children's Books, 2002.

MacLachlan, Patricia. *All the Places to Love*. New York: HarperCollins, 1994.

Polacco, Patricia. *Thunder Cake*. New York: Philomel Books, 1990.

Rylant, Cynthia. *Birthday Presents*. New York: Orchard Books, 1987.

Rylant, Cynthia. *The Relatives Came*. New York: Atheneum Books for Young Readers, 2001.

Woodson, Jacqueline. *The Other Side*. New York: G.P. Putnam's Sons, 2001.

Woodson, Jacqueline. *Sweet, Sweet Memory*. New York: Hyperion, 2000.

Books with strong examples of change:

Bridges, Margaret Park. *I Love the Rain*. San Francisco, CA: Chronicle Books, 2005.

Child, Lauren. *I Will Never Not Ever Eat a Tomato*. Cambridge, MA: Candlewick Press, 2003.

Polacco, Patricia. *Pink and Say*. New York: Philomel Books, 1994.

Polacco, Patricia. *Thank You, Mr. Falker*. New York: Philomel Books, 1998.

Polacco, Patricia. *Thunder Cake*. New York: Philomel Books, 1990.

Reynolds, Peter H. *The Dot*. Cambridge, MA: Candlewick Press, 2003.

Viorst, Judith. *Alexander, Who's Not (Do You Hear Me? I Mean It!) Going to Move*. New York: Aladdin Paperbacks, 1995.

Viorst, Judith. *Alexander and the Terrible, Horrible, No Good, Very Bad Day*. New York: Aladdin Paperbacks, 1972.

Woodson, Jacqueline. *The Other Side*. New York: G.P. Putnam's Sons, 2001.